Schema
OF A SOUL

Schema OF A SOUL

KIMBERLYE BERG

Schema Press
LINCOLN, NEBRASKA

Printed in the United States of America

Schema Press

ISBN 978-0-615-84846-4

10 9 8 7 6 5 4 3 2 1
First Edition Printing October 2013

Cover design, page design, and typesetting by Megan Berg.
Chapter sketches by Jim Berg.

For Jim

Contents

What others are saying

"*Schema of a Soul* is a poetic, literary masterpiece. Kim Berg's command of the English language will navigate readers through a visual journey of love, profound loss, overwhelming pain, and eventual hope. The story comes alive in a kaleidoscope of color, bringing the reader along as a passenger on a sojourn through dark places of grief and light-filled places of hope and faith.

Schema of a Soul challenged many of my preconceived notions about how humans are supposed to navigate grief. Pastors, counselors, social workers, anyone who has experienced the grief that comes with the death of a child or loved one—this book is a must-read. Grief writes its own unique schematic on each one's soul. Kim Berg's powerful narrative will challenge and encourage readers from many walks of life regarding the importance of acknowledging and allowing that unique schematic to be written during overwhelming grief and loss."

—JON STANTON
Author and Speaker, hopefortheheavy.com

When the raging winds of pain blow, we yearn for a safe shelter for our souls. The beautiful tapestry of practical and spiritual connections woven in *Schema of a Soul* wrap securely around the reader, offering connection where there is isolation, vision where there is chaos, and faith where there is doubt. Whether you seek to understand and comfort those who mourn or you are aware of your own pain, nestle in. And may sacrificial love demonstrate the truth of its strength in you.

—ANDREA WENBURG
M.A. Counseling Ministries

"If there is any interest in sharing favor, approval or placing your hand in the small of someone's back to be a support... now is the time to give this blessing to Kim Berg for authoring *Schema of a Soul*. The exposure of real-life grief and love is raw and tangible. You may need to be warned that God will take you to places you will never ask to go to on your own and cover you with layers of grace and mercy you may never feel again. *Schema of a Soul* will waken you to a description of grief that many moms, wives, and friends have had to fight for as they learn to breathe again on their own after the death of their own child. I thank God for this private and intimate insight to life."

—JACKIE J. BATES
Author of *Conversations: Living Through the Process of Dying*

Foreword

For years, the tall black boots with just the right heel stood in my closet marking the before and after.

Before, Kim and I went to lunch and perused the January sales. I tried on the boots. Kim said I would wear them forever. She also told me she was feeling uneasy about a trip two of her kids would leave on the next day. I probably said something trite like, "It will be okay." Or, "I'll pray for you."

Then Saturday came and a car tumbled off an embankment and relationships tumbled into pain and chaos.

After, Kim chose a deep, lonely path into the heart of brokenness. I would like to say I went with her, that I understood her need to live in the grief for a long, long time. After, I was impatient. I was afraid.

We never know what to say when tragedy interrupts life. I thought I knew more than others because I had grown up in a family shaped by the sudden death of a child. What I didn't know was the depth of my own unwillingness to enter into another's pain.

After, it would be a long time before lunches and shopping and sharing our fears, yet a tenuous thread of grace kept us connected. We would both need forgiveness. We would both need to forgive.

Nine years after that Saturday, Kim and I sat in a coffee shop. Kim was churning with a book she wanted to write for

Jim. I was filled with ideas and projects as I transitioned back into the life of full-time freelance work. We made Wednesdays our day to meet and to write. Slowly, we emerged as writers and as friends with a past, and— this is the best part— a future.

I was overwhelmed and honored as Kim read those first paragraphs to me in her quiet, strong voice. As the pages, then chapters emerged, I sensed that Kim's story would be important not just for her and Jim and for me, but for all who have attempted to shield their hearts from pain. This is not a light book to lay on the night stand and read as you fall asleep. This book will shake your soul awake, if you will let it.

The boots are gone. I wore them for a decade, which is forever in shoe years. I still think about them and about the before and the after.

Thank you, Kim, for sharing your journey and for inviting me into an after that is exceedingly rich and deep and beautiful.

Your Before and After Friend,
Cindy

Preface

Dear Reader,

I have written *Schema of a Soul*, in particular, as an offering of love to my husband, Jim. I speak directly to him throughout the story.

However, I could not write **Schema of a Soul** *without also talking to God. A vastly layered love story, I want it to be an offering to Him as well. If it were not for Him, this story would have a significantly different ending. I would have a significantly different ending.*

I hope the delineation of font styles will keep the story flowing in a way that will be engaging for you rather than confusing.

My most meaningful relationships have, paradoxically, been the deepest joys and the deepest sufferings of my life. They are my most magnificent stories of life and death and love.

You have those stories too. They resonate within us all, reverberating what it means to be human. If ever we were to meet for coffee, I would enjoy hearing yours.

Warmly,
Kimberlye Berg

Prelude

*"It is interesting and as difficult
to say a thing well as to paint it.
There is the art of line and colours,
but the art of words exists too,
and will never be less important."*
—Vincent van Gogh

THESE WORDS ARE FOR YOU, JIM, my cherished husband of thirty-three years. They feel very important, and I want you in particular to have them. I have been married to you for many years more than half of my life. I fondly remember the day we met at the tender ages of fourteen and seventeen—in the high school library of our hometown. We introduced ourselves in quiet voices standing at the well-worn wooden newspaper rack.

I was much more intrigued by the story in your face than that of the headlines.

As I reminisce over the memory of how we met, I responsively enjoy another library. The library you have artistically designed and built for me.

Story surrounds me.

Soothes and disturbs me.

From my desk by the window surrounded by my favorite books, old typewriters, and cameras, I look out into the terrace. I see a white, blooming dogwood tree. It stands

like an elegant umbrella, offering a quiet, protected place
to think. There is a memorial bench tucked in like a hug at
the base of its trunk. Twinkling garden lights like warm-
hearted smiles accentuate its beauty, inviting us to enjoy
its deeply rooted aliveness.

Ferns of asparagus and Boston, surrounded by coco-
nut moss, wave their fronds at me like old, favorite friends.
The asparagus has tiny white flowers falling down all around
and plump, pastel green berries. Window boxes burst with
English ivy, white impatiens, and cascading verbena.

Ambitious woodbine creeps confidently toward the
sun, fabricating walls of foliage—layer upon layer of texture and multiple shades of green with bright red stems. Its
varying sizes of five-pointed leaves in all stages of growth
play hide-and-seek with the wind and the sun, making me
want to play too.

I joyfully anticipate the way green will turn to deep
golds and reds, exploding with big blue berries in the fall. I
envy the anxious way it explores new directions, sharing its
luscious, alive beauty as it flourishes thick and vigorous. It
will make me sad when the leaves fall, leaving the stems
bare and exposed. I will eagerly await its blooming beauty
when it bursts out all over again in the spring.

Majesty palms wave their willowy branches beck-
oning us to share their sheltered space. I hear the bubbling
calm of the fountain, memory stones thoughtfully collected
and placed in the water. There are so many things I never
want to forget.

Quartal mezzo chimes move spontaneously with the
wind, improvising a stream of euphonious melodies. Living
things sense the rhythm and eagerly join the chorus of graceful movements. The hammered copper table surrounded
by chairs and candles has been a mooring of many lively
conversations. Encircled by the walls of our home, this is

an entirely private space. It feels like an actual room, but it is all outside, and we can see the sky.

A quote, spoken by Friedrich von Schelling, at the entrance to our house reads: *"Architecture in general is frozen music."* I marveled in watching you design this home for us. I wonder, after having traveled a particularly rough road, if you had any idea as you sketched every drawing by hand on the antique drafting table you inherited from your son—who laboriously restored every inch of it—how much your professional intuition was to meld with your personal. You are director of a symphony of spaces. Consolingly thoughtful places to be. To connect. To laugh. Cry. Think. Enjoy. Celebrate. Work. Play. Rest. Create. Invite. Sing. Dance. Live. To be together.

I live... in frozen music. Your offering is so beautiful to me. I long to give beautiful back to you. Can I find words to express such poignant sentiments that have permeated my life with you, unveiling story I could never have anticipated?

I feel the music. I sense with anticipatory delight your movement toward me.

We, along with our stories, have become entwined, leading us into the most intimate experiences and expressions of relational dance. We have danced to requiems and odes. We have danced amongst the harmony of consonance and the harshness of dissonance. We have danced surrounded by indescribable joy and unimaginable heartache. We have danced in life and in death.

It is a dance of love.

In the beginning, a simple, naive kind of love.

I borrowed my mother's wedding dress. You borrowed your brother's dress shoes. You created an original piece of artwork just for this occasion—a tall wedding banner made of felt to hang at the front of the church we both grew up in. *A man shall cleave unto his wife and the two shall become one. —based on Genesis 2:24.*

Standing at the altar, holding each other's hands and eyes, we spoke our vows out loud, but quietly, to each other. I, Kimberlye, take you James. I consider you, and the meaning of your name as I say it. "Faithful friend." We promise to have and to hold. For better or for worse. For richer or for poorer. In sickness and in health. To love and to cherish until death do us part. I slipped a single band on your finger, pledging all my love in the name of the Father, Son, and Holy Spirit. You slipped three bands on my finger symbolizing the love of Three in One as you pledged yours to me. A modest, so sacred wedding ceremony in our little hometown on the prairie. On a Friday. We two have become one. The beautiful mystery. You, my faithful friend, and I are now bonded together as husband and wife, becoming one flesh, an exclusive relationship neither of us has ever known with anyone else. You are the only one I have ever wanted.

Having said "I do" and sealing it all with a kiss, we exited the church to find a farmer friend dressed in a handsome western black suit with red bolo tie, cowboy hat, and boots, awaiting us with two gorgeous white horses drawing a carriage. You helped me, and my dress, around the massive wooden wheels into the charming carriage with the red-fringed black canopy. He smiled hugely at us and said he would take us wherever we wanted to go. We kissed and hugged and laughed and cried, "I can't believe I get you!" as we clip-clopped all around town.

My mom's church group made salads and sandwiches. We ate at tables set up on my parent's lawn. My dad filled large silver garbage cans with pop and ice. The Avon lady made our wedding cake. We wanted carrot. She had never heard of carrot for wedding cake before, but she made it, beautiful. All I really wanted was you. My brother's band played on the deck. The cousins danced. The giant, bountiful cottonwood trees that grew up with me celebrated too, sprinkling us all with white confetti.

Having enjoyed celebrating our wedding with family and friends, and the carrot cake, we hugged everyone good-bye. Anxious to make stories of us—Mr. and Mrs.—we loaded our fresh promises, hopes, dreams, and our enraptured selves into our 1963 aqua-colored Ford Fairlane. It had wings near the taillights. It did not have seat belts. Even today I get goose bumps when you say "my wife."

We, you and me—Mr. and Mrs.—started down the uncertain road.

With our untried vows.

Our untested love.

Thirty-three years later, love is no longer simple or naive.

What is it?

Written randomly throughout our walls are words of wisdom from people who challenge and inspire us. In our sitting room, a contemplative thought voiced by Aldous Huxley reads: "*After silence, that which comes nearest to expressing the inexpressible is Music.*" Words with meanings big enough can be hard to find. I imagine I will find some of the words. Others will elude me. Nonetheless, this composed construction of words is my offering to you.

May you hear the music in the silence of the space between the lines when the words are insufficient. It is a song of my profound, dying-then-undying love. For you. My dearly beloved.

—Kim

Saturdays at Six

ONE

"The way to love anything is to realize it might be lost."
—G. K. Chesterton

MY BODY TELLS ME WHEN IT is Saturday. Six o'clock p.m. It always knows. It has never forgotten.

The violent blast. A destructive wave of highly compressed air—squeezing and pressing and flattening it—like it was taking up too much space. I wondered how so much, *much too much,* could be squeezed and pressed and flattened in the space of so little time.

The suffocating dust clouds of fine powder. Carried by the tainted air, consisting of millions of tiny particles of disbelief; my lungs could barely breathe them in.

The gravitational force. Pulling, pulling, pulling its critical structural connections toward the center of the earth. Fighting with a severe, solemn surge of strength my body had never felt before, I fell to the floor.

The bursting inwards. Of anguish. Agony. Torment. Stabbing pain. Severe sadness. A raw aching.

The violent inward collapse. Of life as it had known it. Of the life I had known.

The implosion. Of me.

Saturday. 19 January 2002. Six o'clock p.m. The phone rang.

"Mrs. Berg? You need to come right away. There has been an accident. We need permission to treat your daughter."

My heart sank. I had no idea how far it was to fall.

The phone rang again. You answered to hear Megan's voice. Megan's alive voice. Alive with the pain in her body and the pain in her heart. How much pain can a fifteen-year-old body and heart hold?

"Didn't they tell you? Michael and Courtney are dead." How does a daughter tell her dad that his son and his son's girlfriend are dead? How did she tell you? What words did she find for you, lying there with her broken places in a hospital bed? Talking to a chaplain. Not talking to her brother, who had stories yet to live and breathe with her. Only he wasn't living. He had stopped breathing.

What words from your father-heart did you find for her, standing there in the ordinariness of our kitchen—holding only the phone?

The pain in her body will get better. The pain in her heart will just keep coming.

You turned to tell me.

The squeezing. The pressing. The flattening. The suffocating. The disbelief. The pulling. The fighting. The falling. The bursting. The violent inward collapse.

I remember the feel of your yellow starched shirt. I remember the agony written in your blue eyes. Familiar eyes that I can read like a well-loved history book. I remember your white face. I remember leaning against the tiled kitchen wall and falling to the wood parquet floor.

Your strong yellow arms came to me on the floor.

What color of strong is strong enough to hold all of this?

The phone rang again. You answered to hear the doctor's voice. "I'm sorry it was your daughter who told you your son is dead. Come. As soon as you can."

I hate it when the phone rings.

Michael had called just a short time earlier to tell me they were safe and having a wonderful time. They were looking forward to the dinner theater at the Iron Springs Chateau that evening. We talked and laughed. Unknowingly, we spoke *last words* to each other. Last laughs. Last sentiments. The most-recent-in-time words now seem very-distant-past words. We will get no more words. Or time. The soothing voice of Enya singing *Only Time* had filled their car. If only we had more time. We have no more time.

It is gone.

He is gone.

Seldom can you know what time last words will come to you. All words hold the potential of being last words. Trauma brings with it an acute awareness of the complexity of time. Of no time. Time becomes nebulous, disjointed, separated from what is seemingly the regular course of the day. Ordinary life is ruptured by the extraordinary. We typically live passively centered in chronos time: the ordinary, chronological, tick-tock of the clock kind of time that quantitatively measures our days. I am feeling the intense impact of kairos time: the extraordinary holy-overwhelming-interruption-God-given kind of time of a qualitative nature. What is time to God? What is eternal? What is temporal? Life is not linear or orderly or neat and tick-tock-tidy. There is no way to quantitatively measure all of the days, all of the time, all of the words that have been lost except by the qualitative magnitude of the hole left behind.

I am flailing in a huge hole.

Flailing in the intense interruption.

According to the chronos clock, thirty minutes after our last words Michael was dead.

How do you measure thirty minutes?

How can it be possible that the cell phone attached to Michael's body continued to rhythmically flash its green light, indicating that it was still on—but his heart was not beating? No rhythmic pattern at all: he was dead.

Remember? Just the night before? How he burst into our room laughing, talking, flopping down on top of us, chatting away? His phone was attached to his belt like always. The green light was blinking.

His heart was beating.

My heart is throbbing.

I hate it when the phone doesn't ring.

I have a distinct memory of standing next to the antique library table in the golf room on that fateful morning, saying to you, "I am not sure why, but it feels like a creepy day. I wish we could start it all over again."

If only we could.

The not-so-charming pink-and-blue flowered paper that disgraced our family room came with the so charming brick Cape Cod house on the quaint, tree-lined street. The day I picked the flowers off the walls and put up a traditional Scottish plaid-patterned paper was the day our children officially dubbed it "the golf room."

We were obscurely aware that the enjoyment we found in collecting antique wooden golf clubs and historical golf books was not so much that we were collectively crazy about all things golf. We knew you were absolutely crazy about all things golf, and we were absolutely crazy about you. Since our wedding day, "I can't believe I get you!" has been an endearing family mantra. While occasionally expressed in tones of sarcasm, an underlying affection prevails. We wanted to celebrate you—the man we love. Over the years those plaid walls came to hold the stories of us more than they held the story of golf.

Then came the creepy day.

During breakfast we had planned a valentine's fondue party for when we would all be together again. The kids headed for Colorado. I headed for an estate sale.

Hardwood floors had just been installed in the charming Cape Cod. Not one thing escaped the dust and disarray caused by this invasive home improvement project. Having such a massive cleaning project in front of me, I should not have been out gallivanting at an estate sale.

What is it that draws any of us to estate sales anyway? Estate sales beg the question "Is this what it comes to?" Years of collecting historical golf treasures, all to end up in an estate sale.

I have collected antique books since I was a young girl. More fodder for the estate sale that would be ours. As I hold them in my hands I ponder whose hands have held them before me, where in the world they have traveled over the years, who originally bought them, gave them, received them, and why. I marvel over the kind of paper that was chosen, the printing process, and the art that graces the covers. Each book holds a story all its own.

An estate sale itself begs a story to be told. Someone in this particular house also collected antique books. I could not believe what treasures of story I discovered and would be able to purchase for just a few dollars. Aren't they worth much more? *Life of William McKinley and Complete Story of His Assassination*, written in 1901, the year in which it happened, by Marshall Everett and *Illustrious Life of William McKinley Our Martyred President*, also written in 1901 by Murat Halstad.

Inside the cover is written: *"The true story, in the shadow of death, passing away, funeral ceremonies; It is God's way; His will, not ours, be done."* The more-than-one-hundred-year-old books are beautiful works of art.

All of a sudden in the mass of people crowding along a steep staircase, an older gentleman was falling down the stairs. He was lying at the bottom stair, not moving. Someone needed to call 911. So I did. The operator told me to keep him still; they would be there right away. No one would listen to me. They kept trying to make him get up.

I could have no idea that in just a few hours another woman would find herself in a place where a car with three people inside had just violently rolled six times down a steep embankment, totally crushing it.

Someone needed to call 911. So she did.

The shadow of death. Funeral ceremonies. It is God's way,

not ours. His will, not ours, be done. What does that mean? I wonder where the eerie euphemistic phrase "passing away" came from. Passing away? The combination of the words *pass* and *away* feel strange. Maybe it bothers me because it feels like trying to make death sound more polite. Palatable. Death is not polite. It is certainly not palatable. Death will not be softened by favorable representations. Our son has not passed away. He is dead.

Dead. What a strange-sounding word.

How is it these stories of death ended up in my hands on the day our firstborn son was to die? That I would call 911 for an injured gentleman. But I could do nothing to help my own.

You went upstairs to tell Tyler. He was so quiet. I wondered what was going on inside of him. You have some idea, don't you? I remember the day your brother Brad died at age nineteen. I felt helpless as you struggled to make sense of it. Today—on the nineteenth day of the New Year—your son has died at age nineteen. You, your father-brother love shaped in the fire of knowing your brother and not knowing your father, will be strong and tender for your son whose only brother has died.

Before thirty minutes had passed we started down the same road the kids had traveled that day. How can the familiar look so strange?

It was getting dark. How congruous was that. It was getting dark all right.

It would be dark for a long time.

"Last times" began to hinder my respiration. Breathing seemed to come naturally just an hour ago. Now I had to remind myself. Breathe. Breathe. Breathe. My mind swims in chaos. Would it be worse if both Michael and Megan had died? I cannot even imagine. How could it be worse? How could it not be worse? It would be *more* of the worst. How much "more" would there be yet to come? Which one of us would die next? If it is not me, I am going to be really ticked. Selfishly, I cannot imagine more of this kind of pain. I cannot imagine life—without you.

We need to contact a mortuary. Which one should we call?

I have never thought about planning a funeral for our children. Have you?

Funeral. What a strange-sounding word. From the Latin *funus*. Meaning "death." A ceremony honoring a dead person, typically involving interment: the burial of a corpse in a grave or a tomb. Corpse. What a strange-sounding word. Indicating that a change has occurred—a human body that is no longer alive but dead.

We drive through the night in numbing shock and begin to wonder about Michael's funeral. We want to tell stories with words and music. One of the stories we will tell is of Horatio G. Spafford, an attorney who lived in Chicago. In 1871 he lost a financial fortune in the great Chicago fire. That could not compare with the death of his four-year-old son due to scarlet fever around the same time. In 1873 he planned to take his wife and three daughters on a restorative vacation to Europe. An urgent matter caused him to send them on ahead with his promise to join them as soon as possible.

While they slept in the night, their ship collided with an iron sailing vessel in the icy ocean.

Michael was born on November 22.

Horatio and Ann Spafford's three young daughters all died on November 22.

Ann cabled her husband: "Saved alone." He rushed to join her. The ship captain called to Mr. Spafford in his cabin as they passed over the place in the sea where his daughters had died. He later penned the words to the hymn *It Is Well with My Soul*. We will join hands with our family and friends at Michael's funeral, and we will sing *It Is Well with My Soul*.

Waves of more. Of the Worst. When sorrows like sea billows roll and roll…

Is it well with my soul?

You know this place, don't You, God?

I want to know You. In this place.

How will we know Your suffering if we don't enter into our own suffering?

I held tightly to Michael's favorite soft leopard blanket, although it did not stop the chills running down my spine. Everything felt so unnatural. Unearthly. It was like we were in a capsule. Catapulting into very dark darkness.

We arrived at the hospital—located on Lincoln Street, the same name as the city we live in. I could not get to Megan fast enough. I looked into her eyes. One of them was not her normal big, beautiful blue, same as you, but all red and filled with blood. I hope it is not as bad as it looks, that it will be well again. Will she be well again?

I began to hug her, only it hurt her. Holding hands was the most we could manage without inflicting more pain. To see her … hear her … be with her. Michael and Courtney had been taken to a mortuary a few miles down the road.

I wanted to go with you to meet the coroner. To go to the car. Collect their things. To see the car would be very difficult. I wanted to see Michael. Much more difficult—but they wouldn't let us. They wouldn't let us? I wanted to do everything together, but that was not possible. The doctor was coming to talk to us at the same time. I stayed to meet with him. I saw the coroner handing you Michael's phone. I heard him tell you he had turned off the green blinking light.

I struggled to look into the doctor's face, listen to his voice, and take notes on his instructions about how to take care of Megan and her injuries all at the same time. Where was my mind? In so many places. I felt terribly distracted. The nurse graciously insisted I try to eat some soup. I could barely look at it. I was going to throw up any minute. Just as graciously, she took it away. My aunt and uncle, a few friends, my brothers and sister had come. Meeting them in the corridor, I leaned against the wall trying to stay vertical but had to slide my way down the wall to the floor, trying not to faint.

My body was working hard amongst its own parts to keep things functioning. It has never forgotten, and so reminds me.

On Saturdays at six.

Sometimes, I still have to lean against the wall.

Saturdays at Six

TWO

✑

*"You can only find truth with logic if you have
already found truth without it."*

—G. K. Chesterton

THE MEMORY OF GETTING BACK IN the car to go home haunts me. We reclined a seat and placed a thick piece of foam on it in an attempt to make the four hundred miles more comfortable for Megan. Comfort did not come in any form. The surprises that Michael and Courtney had planned in contagious excitement remain forever secret from her. The dinner theater. The Cheyenne Mountain Zoo. The cog rail up Pike's Peak. Exploring Colorado College where Courtney was in her junior year. Feeding ducks at the pond nearby. Hiking in Garden of the Gods. Pizza and combing the used books at Poor Richard's.   A friend gave Megan a valentine teddy bear as we left the hospital. I thought of the valentine fondue party we had planned. Michael and Courtney will not be there.

They will not be at anything anymore.

We stopped at the Rite Aid Pharmacy drive-through for prescription pain medicine costing only $17.98. If only it *could* take away the pain.

Maybe we could just keep driving. Driving forever and ever. There is no place like home, but it will never be the same. Home has changed forever.

We have changed forever.

Part of us has died too.

When we arrived, the house was filled with people, food, and flowers. So many flowers. Reports of the accident were all over the news.

We rested in Michael's bed that night, though sleep did not come. I pulled the sheets and blanket up around my face, keeping his scent as close to me as possible. People die every day. All around the world. *People in general* feels very different than *people in particular*. Particularly people that I have given birth to. Uniquely formed in love, the fusing of your cells and mine into a whole new life with a name. A heart. A soul.

A relentless yearning tugged at me—unmercifully—to be where Michael was. I wanted to be near his body. I did not want to leave him at the mortuary in Colorado, to go home without him. What else were we to do? I wonder what the room looked like where he was. I wish I could have been there with him, stayed right beside him, but that was not possible. There were decisions we needed to make in regard to his body between two mortuaries in two states. I want to clearly comprehend our choices, but everything feels incomprehensible in the moment.

Having wrestled our way through the night, first thing the next morning we met with the funeral director. Otherwise known as the undertaker. How did they ever come to be called undertaker? In the fourteenth century that was simply someone who accepted responsibility for the performance of any certain task. By 1698 funeral undertaker had become common—the perfect euphemism for arranging funerals. In the late nineteenth century undertakers in the United States decided that was a rather gloomy word. Preferring something more professional, they combined the Latin root *mort*, meaning "death," with *physician*, thereby calling themselves morticians. It seems funeral director is now the preferred term, although not all funeral directors are licensed to embalm, in which case one might delineate themselves as a mortician.

Embalm. What a strange-sounding word. From the Old French *embaumer*. It means to preserve and protect a corpse from change and decay with fragrant spices. Today injections of preservatives are used

instead of spices. Ancient Egyptians developed a process of preserva-
tion, lasting around seventy days, that would essentially mummify a
body because they believed the soul would return to the corpse.

Embalming methods advanced substantially in the United
States during war due to the fact that many servicemen were dying
far from home and their families wanted the bodies returned home
for burial. When President Abraham Lincoln's body was embalmed,
enabling him to be sent home for burial, it brought considerable attention to the embalming process, making it much more widespread. In
1867 German chemist August Wilhelm von Hofmann discovered form-
aldehyde, which became the basis for current methods of embalming.

After extracting all of the blood and intestinal fluids from the
body, there are essentially four parts to this process, which takes several
hours to complete. Beginning with arterial embalming, chemicals are
injected into blood vessels. Massaging of the body can be necessary to
break up circulatory clots in order for the fluid to distribute properly
to all areas. The next procedure entails making a small incision above
the navel. The hollow organs are punctured, the contents aspirated,
then chemicals are injected to fill the cavities. Hypodermic embalming is injecting chemicals with needle and syringe into tissue to even
everything out.

Powders are applied to the body to attempt to mask odors. Eyes
are kept closed by applying a sticky sort of cream. The jaw is often tied
together with suture string. Then there is the "setting of the features."
Where they use cosmetics to fix your face and spray to fix your hair.
To make you look not so dead. Familiar. Like you looked before.

But nothing is as it was before.

The law requires autopsies of all car accident fatalities. To
think I was just outside the door when Michael had his wisdom teeth
removed, but I will be nowhere near when he has an autopsy. In an
autopsy the organs are removed—irreversibly disrupting the circulatory system—making the embalming procedures somewhat different
and more difficult.

Will the human being who holds Michael's heart, in their
hands, feel how big it is? How tender and warm it is? This heart of his
that was formed and beat for the first time with fetus life inside of me.

Umbilically connected, we shared circulatory systems.

Blood.

Life.

My circulatory system is irreversibly disrupted too.

I am struggling. This all feels very disturbing to me. Entirely unnatural. If we are going to bring Michael's body across the state line, law requires he must be embalmed.

If you believe your soul will return to your dead body, I suppose you would go to great lengths to make certain your body would be available. Extracting what was the lifeblood coursing through one's veins while alive and replacing it with chemicals seems irreverent somehow. I wonder what is done with the extracted blood. It feels strange and surreal.

Everything has changed, and there is absolutely nothing spices or preservatives can do about it.

Our alternative is cremation. The body is placed in basically a cardboard box with a plywood bottom, called a cremation casket. Then into a cremation chamber known as a retort. Latin, from the verb *retorquere*. Meaning "in return." Twisted back or cast back. Perhaps a reference to dust to dust, ashes to ashes? The chamber heats up to about two thousand degrees Fahrenheit. The process takes about two hours. Then there is a cool-down period of about thirty minutes. A handheld magnet is used to go through the remains in order to take out metal pieces, such as fillings. Bone fragments are pulverized in something similar to a blender. Combined, this is known as cremains. More commonly known as ashes.

Do you feel confronted? I feel so confronted. The question of whether we embalm Michael's body or have it cremated matters little, I suppose. It is the question of Death taunting its hostile way, staring us straight in the face, that matters more.

How will we walk through the fire?

Our own internal combustion?

Will it be well with our souls?

What of us will survive the flames?

We decide to have Michael's body cremated there and then

sent home, eliminating embalming issues. Michael's body would not have been easily embalmed anyway. There is some concern he will not be home in time for his own funeral.

We request air express.

Most of me wishes I could be the one to care for my dead child. To prepare him for burial. To wrap him in a shroud and place him in a grave. But they wouldn't even let me see him. It is I who will be wrapped in a shroud. A shroud of sorrow. The professionals will be handling my son's body instead.

I am grappling with the way our culture deals with death, dead bodies, and burial. Families used to care for their dead. Small graveyards used to be an integral part of neighborhoods. Now we have funeral home corporations and massive cemeteries. Many require all the same grave markers, flat to the ground, in order to make mowing the grass easier. Plastic flowers are preferred because fresh ones make too much of a mess, causing cleanup issues.

We discuss the death certificate. There are basically four sections to a death certificate. Decedent. Disposition. Certifier. Cause of death. The language is clinical and formal. Place of death. Time of death. Date pronounced dead. Manner of death. What a strange thing. A legal document to declare and certify death.

In the middle of the director's questions, I have one of my own. "What do you like about your job?" "Helping people," he answers, seemingly unfazed by my unsolaced frankness. He is likely used to strange social behavior regarding such unpleasant matters by those of us referred to as the bereaved. What a strange-sounding word. Bereaved. Robbed by death. Deprived of a loved one through a profound absence.

I find myself experiencing an entirely new language. Perhaps it is not the language that is new as much as the energy of the reality behind it. I do not like the word bereaved.

I am determined to live through the death of our son as fully alive as I can.

We pass through an enormous room of caskets. I experience a strange kind of flashback to my childhood while walking between them. My parents owned a grocery store. We kids basically grew up there. We shared an enormous garage with the neighbor next door—the funeral home. Grocery freight and dead bodies were delivered through the same garage door. Caskets lined the walls of the giant garage. I remembered a time of feeling deeply sad—passing through that cavernous space and wishing I could climb into one of those caskets.

Just disappear.

Today is a despondently new level of sad. A depth I have never, ever known. I feel the urge to pick one.

Any one.

Climb in.

Close the lid.

Disappear.

I resist the forceful urge and keep walking instead.

I am very aware of your gentle strength permeating the space beside me.

Another flashback pops into my head. I am with you at the funeral home next door to the grocery store. It is your senior year in high school. The father you never knew, since he left his family when you were two years old and your mother was pregnant with their eleventh child, had just been found dead while custom combining somewhere in the Midwest. The funeral director would not let you, or your younger brother Brad, see your father's body. You really wanted to. The only time you had vaguely seen him in your whole life was walking down Main Street with an older brother a year earlier. As you crossed at the four-way stop in our little town, your brother told you that you had just passed by your father. Did he not see you?

I wonder what thoughts were going on inside of him as he just kept walking. How could you father eleven children and not know them if you passed them on the street? I wonder what thoughts were going on inside of you.

Finally the funeral director relented. You got to at least see what your father looked like dead. I remember his funeral as being very sad because no one was very sad. I wonder if his casket was one of those that lined the garage.

I wonder what your father thought about when he was all alone with his thoughts. I wonder if he could have had any idea how much he missed in not knowing you. I knew your mother. I wonder what it was in him that she fell in love with. It must have been something beautiful before alcohol made it ugly. I wonder what his last words were. I wonder who he said them to.

We enter into the small room that displays the urns. Another strange word. Urn. Otherwise known as bone pot or ossuary. A vessel used for preserving the ashes or fossilized bones of the dead.

Our son is the dead.

I have another question for the funeral director. "Is there anything special about these urns? Are there governmental requirements they must meet?" "No," he says. Good. We will not be choosing any of these. They need new urn designers, I think to myself. We will find one on our own. We thank the funeral director for his kindness on our way out, and we really mean it.

Being amongst all of the urns and caskets feels so unnatural. Inorganic. Clinical. Funerals are a twenty-five-billion-dollar-a-year business in the United States. On average a single funeral costs between seven and nine thousand dollars. On this day it will not be business as usual. On this day I will be the undertaker. I will undertake responsibility for this certain task as much as I am allowed. I am feeling the intense difference between *in general* and *in particular*. I will not be using formal words like decedent. Or corpse. Or bereaved. Or urn. We will write our own obituary, although we must give it to the funeral director, and he will give it to the newspaper office so they know it is not a joke. I would have never thought of that. Who does that?

Obituary.

Another strange word. A short biographical account of a deceased person.

This "deceased person" is an alive story in spite of the fact that he is dead.

Saturdays at Six

THREE

❧

YOU HAD MY BACK, LITERALLY. With no wall to lean against I sat on a stool and leaned into you. Your strengthening hands on my shoulders, I read a letter at Michael's funeral I had written to him earlier, which included the C. S. Lewis quote I love so much from his book *The Four Loves*.

> There is no safe investment. To love at all is to be vulnerable. Love anything, and your heart will certainly be wrung, and possibly broken. If you want to make sure of keeping it in tact, you must give your heart to no one, not even an animal. Wrap it carefully round with hobbies and little luxuries; avoid all entanglements; lock it up safe in the casket of your selfishness. But in that casket - safe, dark, motionless, airless, it will change. It will not be broken. It will become unbreakable, impenetrable, irredeemable. The only place outside heaven where you can be perfectly safe from all the dangers of love is hell.

Michael was an intense and passionate person. He felt and thought things deeply. He understood, to some degree, what C. S. Lewis meant. He wisely chose unsafe investments. I got to be one of them. So did you. We watched him live the struggle. Fight for safety or embrace brokenness?

Eighteen years old, six feet, four inches tall, wearing blue jeans and his favorite wool sweater, Michael stood in the doorway to the kitchen—his long, skinny fingers wrapping the top of the trim board. I sat at the table admiring his thick brown hair, his expressive blue eyes. Just like yours.

"Mom!" he said, brimming with emotion. "I am so broken. Can't you just fix me?" He placed his index finger on the bridge of his glasses, like he did often, pushing them farther up on his nose, and looked at me intently.

"All around me there is brokenness. Buildings, buses, and people. Everything around me seems so broken. Even me." It had been a harsh week around the world. The school bus crash on I-80. The suicide bomber attack that blew up a café full of people drinking coffee the day before. The man from North Korea who packed himself in a cargo crate trying to get to America but died during the ship's long passage. A close friend of Michael's in the military had just returned from the Middle East. Having survived serving in Iraq, he came home to be hit by a car while riding his bicycle, causing a severe brain injury. He remained in a coma. Michael had been following right behind him when the accident occurred.

Michael described what he was feeling as a "crippling epiphany." He was seeing difficult and disturbing things about life he had not seen before.

We meandered next door into the golf room. We squeezed into the giant wing chair covered in a deep green tapestry of golf courses from around the world and chatted by the fire. We considered what Jean Valjean (Victor Hugo) might have meant as we read his words from *Les Miserables* I had stenciled on the wall nearby: *"He who does not weep does not see."*

As our conversation regarding the ultimate meaning of life unfolded, we concluded that you couldn't fully appreciate the answer unless you fully appreciate the profundity of the question. What is the answer? Is there one?

There is so much we do not see.

Tell me, Michael, what is it that makes you cry? What is it that you see?

I want to see you.

Something alluring was going on in Michael, and it did not

need fixing. I felt so drawn into this conversation. I felt so drawn—to him.

The struggle feels more intense than ever now that he has died. "*When you know and when you love you shall suffer still. The day dawns in tears. The luminous weep, were it only over the dark.*" —Victor Hugo.

The giant wing chair covered in the deep green tapestry of golf courses from around the world feels blisteringly lonely as I curl up in it all by myself. Seeing difficult and disturbing things about life I had not seen before. My own "crippling epiphany."

I begin to see more profoundly the profundity of the question. And I weep.

What is it that You see, God?

I want to see you.

Where are you?

Courtney's parents had discovered a beautiful wooden box for her ashes. They placed a laser-cut photograph of Courtney and Michael on the front of it. We chose the same for Michael.

Cards stuffed our mailbox. I read them late at night when all of you had gone to sleep. I especially enjoyed stories that expressed how others had experienced and enjoyed Michael. When they quit coming, I read them all over again. I saved them all.

There was a lot of active commotion right after the accident while preparing for the funeral. People wanted to do practical things to help, and they gave generously to a memorial fund established in Michael and Courtney's names. Ultimately the fund went toward a community effort to construct a building, known as Camelot Commons, at the Children's Zoo, where they had attended a science-focused high school affectionately known as Zoo School. The peacocks were fond of joining them for lunch by the pond. The gibbons freely joined in on conversations, no matter the topic. The mascot is a Bactrian camel named Lot. It is an alive place, conducive for alive learning and growing in community. We thanked everyone for their kindness as genuinely as we knew how.

The day came that you and I went to the location where the accident had happened. The reality of what took place there felt impossible to grasp. A highway patrol officer noticed us and stopped on the side of the road—we introduced ourselves and immediately he knew why we were there. He told us he had been the first emergency person to the scene and about meeting Megan. I am grateful to have met him in person, to look him in the eye and thank him face-to-face for his kindness.

We stepped lightly into the heaviness of the moment. Onto the holy ground. Our tears spilled moisture onto the hard, dry earth. The ground in its grayishness looked to be as desolate as we felt. As we walked around, I recognized Megan's scarf. I found three blue boxes of Michael's favorite Dentyne gum and a tube of Tom's of Maine wintermint toothpaste. It was weird to see items belonging to our children strewn about. You found a CD of Delerium called *Poem*. The jacket cover was weathered but intact. The disc was broken. We will save it with others we found in the car, including U2—*All That You Can't Leave Behind*. I remember the day Michael came home with it, saying, "Mom! Come listen to this song. You have to hear it. It is so beautiful."

I miss the sound of his voice. It was so beautiful. I miss the mess he was always making in creating things. Bits and pieces, parts of taken-apart wholes lay everywhere. Washers, bolts, boards, tools, countless cords of every form, size, and length. Every kind of string known to man. Reams and reams of paper. Miles of duct tape. Old computers prized for their parts cluttered every counter. I miss everything. The good and the not-so good—the mess of us all being alive.

I miss him coming home.

I miss him.

I sat down on the ground. It was harsh and hard.

I wrapped Megan's scarf around my neck. I unwrapped a piece of gum.

I felt so left behind.

Bits and pieces.

Parts of our taken-apart wholes.

Lay everywhere.

The paramedics who responded to the 911 call had given us a bouquet of red silk roses with drops of silicone on them that looked, to me, like tears. They called this spot of land "the hole." They knew when they were called to "the hole" that it was going to be very harsh and very hard.

I scooped up some dirt with my hand. The words *earth* and *ground* come from the Latin *humus*. From the same root as *humus* comes *humilis*, which becomes *humble*, and *humanus*, which becomes *human*. Dust to dust…

I sat in "the hole" holding the dust of the earth in my humbled human hands. Listening to the wind. Turning my fallen face toward the falling sun, I felt the acoustics of the hard and harsh reverberate throughout my being.

I heard the screeching of brakes. Crunching of metal. Enya singing *Only Time*. The shattering of glass. The uncharacteristic scream-ing of our daughter. The rolling of clouds. The rustling of branches. The wailing of sirens. The overwhelming interruption… I heard the panic in the voice of the woman who stopped to help as she called 911. I heard her voice remain calm and comforting as she spoke with Megan.

I heard Michael and Courtney's silence.

We sat there for a long time. We studied the sky. The cedar trees. The sparse vegetation. The lay of the dry land. We surveyed it all.

Poiema is the Greek word meaning "to make," from which the word *poem* derives. Will we walk away from this hard, harsh, holy place carrying both the sorrow of death and the joy of life—making, living, being—a poem of terrible beautiful? A balm of sweet spicy fragrance?

Will it be well with our souls?

I put the dirt in my pocket. Maybe I will add it to Michael's dirt collection. He kept bits of dirt in tiny round containers. In microscopic handwriting he labeled them with the name of the location from which he had collected them.

As a remembrance. Keepsake. Memento. A token from the places he had been.

Saturdays at Six

FOUR

꩜

"We were promised sufferings. They were a part of the program. We were even told, 'Blessed are they that mourn' and I accept it. I've got nothing that I haven't bargained for. Of course, it's different when the thing happens to oneself, not to others, and in reality, not imagination."

—C. S. Lewis

I AM NOT IMAGINING THINGS. THE bursting inward collapse has made a mess of me. I don't think I can clean it up.

Maybe I am not as strong or stable as I thought. All along our way, you, my Architect, have invited me to experience how architecture can both affect and reflect life. What keeps structures stable? Structure is found in nature and architecture. A natural structure is often able to keep itself intact by moving with the external force being imposed upon on it. You tell me that even though architectural structures appear to be rigid or immoveable, you must design for movement. Materials such as steel, glass, even concrete expand and contract with heat.

Will we move with the force, like a tree or a bridge that sways when the strong winds blow? Or will we just break?

Were we designed to allow for movement? Will our souls expand with the heat of troubled times—moving and relating in such a way as to absorb stress and sorrow—revealing something of the character of God within our relationships? Or shrink and collapse in on ourselves in self-absorbed resistant rigidity, demanding that life cooperate with us?

When what I fear the most in life threatens to destroy me, will I survive? What does it mean—really—to survive? Is there anything at the very core of us that cannot be destroyed?

When turbulence comes, can we offer stable strength from our core? Or will we implode? What would that mean in terms of the ways that we are relating with each other?

It terrifies me that there will be more. I am absolutely gripped by terror. Of course there will be more. More pain. More tragedy. More turmoil. More death.

God, I am so broken. Can't you just fix me?

Sorrow has hit me hard in the deepest part of my soul, challenging the way I see, if I see at all, and what I thought I knew about anything and everything. Other people all around the world experience this kind of intense pain and worse. Why not me?

Have my sorrows for them not been as intense as they are for my own?

What does it mean to love each other in this place?

As undertaker, I don't know where to bury Michael. It took us five months to decide. We buried Michael next to Courtney. Her parents will be buried there too.

There is a granite boulder that marks their grave. Their names are engraved into the stone. A diverse collection of small stones representing memories and stories sits on top. We take fresh flowers and bring apples for the squirrels. We make snowmen and snow angels. We blow bubbles.

I'm finding it difficult to be with people. It takes all of my energy. It is hard to focus on anything. My favorite literature and music resound with underlying and pervasive questions and qualities that resonate deep within me and offer some level of solace. A particularly reverberant voice belongs to Asher Lev, created by Chaim Potok. One of many favorite excerpts:

> I remember that the first time I saw the Michelangelo Pietà
> in the Duomo I could not draw it. It was the fifth day of
> July. I stared at its Romanesque and Gothic contours, at the

twisted arm and bent head, at the circle formed by Jesus and
the two Marys, at the vertical of Nicodemus—I stared at
the geometry of the stone and felt the stone luminous with
strange suffering and sorrow. I was an observant Jew, yet
that block of stone moved through me like—like the echoing
blasts of the shofar sounded by the Rebbe. I do not mean to
blaspheme. My frames of reference have been formed by the
life I have lived. I do not know how a devout Christian reacts
to that Pietà. I was only able to relate it to elements of my
own lived past. I stared at it. I walked slowly around it. I do
not remember how long I was there that first time. When I
came back out into the square, I was astonished to discover
that my eyes were wet. (Chaim Potok, *My Name Is Asher Lev*)

I open a book of Michelangelo's art. I ponder the image of the
Pietà, wishing I could snap my fingers and be in St. Peter's Basilica.
Michelangelo, while only in his early twenties, created the Pietà from a
single slab of marble. He depicts, life sized, Mary, the mother of Jesus,
actually holding him in her lap. Grieving over her son, having just
been taken from the cross, before his body was sealed into the tomb. I
wonder... What could be the intrinsic inspiration for this exceptional
young man to sculpt such a tender and sensitive work of art that continues to move so many from all around the world to tears? The Pietà
has been wringing people's hearts for five hundred years. Perhaps it was
that his own mother died when he was just six. Perhaps the anguishing
sorrow depicted in Mary's face is not only her own but a reflection of
his as well.

I feel the intensity of sympathetic vibration echoing and
reechoing in my heart. I imagine being in a conversation with Dr. Potok,
Asher Lev, Michelangelo, and Mary. The sonority of their stories moves
me deeply. A resonance indicating that the frequency in my soulish
circuitry is, at some level, that of the incoming signal.

Longing to hold my firstborn son, I sit in the middle of the
wooden kitchen floor late one night. The night before we are to bury
some of his ashes at Calvary Cemetery. Some. Not all. I am unable to

part with all of them. I turn the mission oak box with the laser picture on the front upside down. I use a Phillips screwdriver to take out four brass screws that allow me access to the ashes inside. I read again the certificate of cremation. It officially certifies these remains are indeed our son's and that all legal requirements have been observed. I tenderly touch the ashes. They are coarse yet powdery. I sit on the wooden kitchen floor and fight desperately to determine what is real. I am trying to comprehend what I can see, while at some level, aware that I simply cannot begin to comprehend what I cannot see. Is what I am able to see the most real? Or what I cannot see?

Perhaps things are not as they seem?

This is my son's body. Unable to actually hold him, I rub his ashes into the skin on the back of my hands and all the way up my arms. Tears mingle with ashes. I kiss them. I place them back in the wooden box. The ache in my ash-covered arms feels heavy with emptiness. My heart pounds mournfully inside me. I can hardly move from this place. I feel profoundly sad that my son has died.

It is late into the night, but sleep does not come to me. The Pietà. The shofar. The ashes. The wooden box. The wooden cross. The sea of death. The river of life. God seems so comforting. God seems so disturbing. These all represent powerful and eloquent stories of life, death, and love. My heart is so moved by them all. I am beginning to see how I relate to each of them in ways I never have before.

Sleepless nights can be long and lonely. I turn on my music, a reverberating embrace of plangent sounds that calm and inspire me. In particular, Brulé's drum. In the Lakota tradition the beat of a drum symbolizes the beat of a heart—the pulsation we have known since inception: the calming beat of a mother's heart to her unborn child.

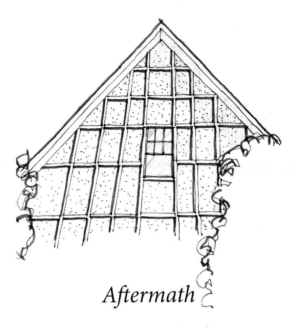

Aftermath

ONE
∽

"Not that I am (I think) in much danger of ceasing to believe in God. The real danger is of coming to believe such dreadful things about Him. The conclusion I dread is not 'So there's no God after all.' but 'So this is what God is really like. Deceive yourself no longer.'"
—C. S. Lewis

I FILLED JOURNALS WITH WORDS AND tears during the toweringly difficult time for our family after Michael died. Several years have now passed, and I recently read through them, which may be a good thing to do. Or not. It is not hard to find myself right back in that wobbly place. At times it can be merciful to forget; however, there is a greater grace-filled mercy in remembering the important impact this part of our story is on the whole of our lives. Hidden heartache has a way of latching itself onto the very atoms of your being, forever becoming a part of you. Sparked by all sorts of sensory impressions, it oozes out, reminding you it is still there, still reforming you.

What a mess we were. Not that we are no longer a mess, but it does bewilder me that we are still married. We hardly spoke to each other for months. I lived in fear. Of everything. *"No one ever told me that grief felt so like fear."* —C. S. Lewis. Most of my illusions and assumptions about whatever I thought I knew about life had been shattered into shreds, but I was still inclined to try to control whatever little bits of life I could. Fear is a scary thing. I panicked over every random siren I heard. I worried when there would be another accident and who of us would die next. Sometimes hope is all that keeps us moving forward, but I was afraid what little hope I might muster was so fragile I would lose it. I could not bear to lose it, again.

You, on the other hand, had become distinctly distant. When you weren't at work, you were working crossword puzzles. The language of your body spoke crosswords. "Do not disturb." Tyler at sixteen was rebelling and in trouble. We told very few people what was going on. I feared the worst. You hoped for the best. I wanted him to have less freedom. You gave him more. Megan at fifteen was struggling. Wondering why she had survived the accident and lived, often wishing she hadn't. All she had seen and been through, and Michael and Courtney being dead, ripped and twisted and tugged at her. At us. I worried about all that ripping inside of her.

Do you remember sitting at the top of the staircase outside her bedroom? We huddled together against the newel post as if it were a firmly fixed footing in a strong storm, crying on each other's shoulders. Listening to her sorrowful sobs on the other side of the door, knowing, for this moment, we needed to let her be alone but wanting to be near.

How we wished we could bear her heavy burden. Something motherly in me wanted to make it better. Something from an even deeper space than motherly instinct knew to think I could somehow make it better would be disrespectful and dismissive of her and her life. What we really want is to be with her in her very deep sorrow.

What does it mean to be with someone whose heart is bleeding and breaking as you are saturated in pain of your own?

What does it mean to love each other in this place?

Jesus in the garden of Gethsemane, on the verge of internal

collapse, was on my mind a lot. It was the only part of the Bible I could read for a very long time. My mourning intensified as I pondered the sorrow and emotional distress tormenting Him. What it must have been like for Him—His own soul sinless, He became sin in order to destroy its power, bearing the weight of the evils of the whole world, including mine. How can we even imagine what this must have been like for Him, and His Father?

Three times Jesus approached His friends to find them sleeping. Unawake. Unalert. Unable to fully grasp the deep mystery in His suffering. Unable to fully grasp Him. Unable to kinetically engage with Him in this holy, lonely place.

Un-, denoting the absence of. Not with. Present, only not present.

Wide-awake-aware, pensively praying not to fall into temptation, Jesus would love them and be with them in ways they did not entirely realize. At the cost of His life.

What does it mean to love each other like that?

I felt overwhelmed by the immensity of tragedy and its life-altering effects. Immersed in my own grievous burdens, I had not wholly entered into each of yours. A devoted part of me, believing God would never leave or forsake us, wanted to be with you in ways that would offer strength, hope, and the kind of love Jesus offered in Gethsemane. A despairing part of me, believing God just doesn't care, was abstractly lost, withdrawn, and hidden in my own heartache.

I was not loving you the way Jesus loves, even as he hung on the cross. I was *un*. The not with. Present, only not present.

About three months after Michael died Tyler left home for three days. He called to let us know he was safe. As he said goodbye he paused, "Mom. I am still here." Safe—as in protected, not exposed to danger or risk—was an illusion that had been shattered and was now a relatively meaningless word to me. But I was not even a safe person for my own son. I had not seen how he wanted and needed me to be with him in ways I was not. I was hearing his anger but not listening to the bundled-up burden beneath it. How could I have not listened to his heart? How could I be so *un*? Not with? It was a startling wake-up call. I wonder—does he wonder if I would cry for him like I have cried for Michael?

We were all tottering in uneasy tension. Quiet introverts, you and I were alone in many ways when we met. In the library. We had never experienced being best friends until we became best friends to each other. Being best friends led to being husband and wife. Now an unfamiliar, heart-wrenching distance settled in between us, threatening to take up permanent residence.

It felt like we had been gutted. Like a building in the midst of an extensive renovation. Important internal parts of us utterly destroyed and ripped out. We were human danger zones, deconstruction underway. Hard hat required, enter at your own risk. Still together, but isolated. Distressed both on the inside and the outside, we seemed alienated from each other and from God. Where was He? He was right there and seemingly did nothing. Where was He now? He did not appear to be present in ways we wanted Him to be.

The strain of such intense disquietude can be shared to some degree, but the hard-to-carry burden must be borne on your own in many ways. I still cried. The tears just came, all the time. Like a burst water pipe that could not be turned off, flooding the already gutted mess, making everything wet and worse. I was unaware of how much my tears bothered you. There is a psalm that speaks of God saving our tears in a bottle. There are so many people all over the world crying. He is going to need really big bottles. What does He do with all of them?

God, what do You do with Yours?

I became very tired of this world and very curious about the next. I felt profoundly sad and so sorry. It seemed like our family was falling apart. I certainly was. I did not know what to do. People all around me kept asking what to do. I don't know. How many times had I answered the phone to hear, "May I speak with your mom?" I would reply with the most authoritative inflection I could manage, "I am the mom."

I am the mom. I should know what to do. Everywhere I look, it hurts. I was so distracted. So tired. So sad. I felt alone. Restless. Unsettled. I couldn't cook or I would throw up. I lost twenty-five pounds and didn't even care. We lived on frozen pizza and Chinese takeout, not that anyone felt much like eating.

Life seemed unbearable at the moment. I wanted relief from the fear that was terrorizing me and the pain that was killing me. Killing me began to sound like a good idea. More than once I considered pulling the car into the garage. Closing the door. I was alone a lot. It would not be hard.

Sorrows. Like sea billows roll. Roll right over me.

It is not at all well with our souls.

Our twenty-second anniversary came. We went out for dinner but got into a terrible conversation. I thought the intense sadness we had been muddling our way through for the last six months would have a tendency to bring us closer together, not tear us apart. In many ways it was the depth of our closeness accumulated over many years that covered a multitude of harsh incidentals. Bound as husband and wife, mother and father, our lives are thoroughly mixed together for better or worse. A commingled spilling of sorrow pressed hard into each of us. It was sorrow upon sorrow to watch each other writhing in so much pain.

What does it mean to love each other in this place?

Sometimes I sensed that you were afraid to let me in, keeping your soul to yourself. What is it like being married to me? You are the only person in the whole world who knows. I have a feeling it is both awful and wonderful.

We asked for our hardly touched meals to be boxed up and went home. I went to bed, but sleep seldom came. You came, an hour later. You had something for me, you said. Red roses and chocolate turtles. You had been giving me chocolate turtles for twenty-seven years. Ever since I met you. In the library. On a card with two glasses of champagne on the front of it, you wrote how you have been mad at me, but you are more mad at God, and you are afraid I am getting the brunt of that. You wrote you hated your life right now, but you don't hate me. The truth is, you love me.

Do you have any idea how much I wanted you to engage with

me like that? How much I wanted you not to be stoic and "soldier" strong but to be real? How much—I wanted *you?*

For the first time in a long time you pulled me right into the heart of you and held me skin-to-skin tight. Something in each of us broke that night as our bodies merged and our tears intermingled, forming a calming emollient, softening us both.

We were so broken, could there be anything left to break? Will we ever feel not so shattered? Weakened fragments of what was and who we were lie scattered about like a broken window. Even if we pick up the pieces somehow, everything is entirely undetermined and rearranged. Nothing will ever be seen or experienced the same way, either outwardly or inwardly, through those particular panes.

Will we move in soul-strengthening ways, with tender affection toward each other as husband and wife? Or will we, two-have-become-one, be unable to find our way together in the labyrinth of inconsolable grief? Stuck in static space, each forming our own favorite freeze-framed images from the past.

Would we ever laugh out loud again? Laugh until we cry. Or will we only know tears of sorrow the rest of our lives? Will life always be so heavy? What will Tyler and Megan's lives be like? How will this change them? What will their relationships be like?

Will serendipitous smiles playfully sneak up on us ever again to radiate into others? Or will they always be controlled, polite, and obligatory?

Will we ever be restored? Regenerated? Redeemed?

It stayed bad at our house for months to come. Some things got worse. We were swirling in a vortex of chaos. The chaos of death. The chaos of life. The chaos of love. Relational turmoil took all of our energy. Never mind the ordinary details of work, school, life.

I paid little attention to the budget. You managed to take care of that along with a myriad of other details. The scolding letters that kept coming from the library caught my impassioned attention. I put the $117 fine in the mail. "Never go anywhere without a few good books," I always said. These books, retrieved from the accident, were now holy remnants. I rub the dirt particles with my fingers and tenderly touch the blood spots.

I watched you struggle with your depression and your heartache while trying to deal with all of the daily demands that were being made on you. When you were particularly sad and stressed, you would disappear.

If I wanted to, I could find you under the covers in Michael's bed.

Getting used to the fact that Michael was gone and not coming back was going to take a while. One day the mortuary that had retrieved Michael's body called to say they had found Michael's wristwatch. They just wanted us to know so we would not be alarmed when it arrived in the mail.

Michael was indeed dead.

A friend of Michael's who had arrived from out of town for a weekend called in hopes of getting together for lunch and a bike ride. I told him Michael could not come.

I told him Michael was dead.

Michael is dead, but I can hear him coming in the side door into the kitchen. The distinct sound of his size fourteen footsteps is one I know and love.

Missing the sound of his voice, I would call Michael's cell phone over and over just to hear his recorded voicemail. Something about that green blinking light infatuated me.

The battery died after just a few weeks and needed to be replaced, so I went to the phone store. I asked the man at the counter for help. He went to find the specific battery from somewhere in the back room, reappeared, and set it on the counter. He laughed, saying, "That's an expensive one—just hand over your firstborn child." I was caught entirely off guard by this familiar colloquialism. He could have no idea that my firstborn child had just died.

I was hoping to simply sign the receipt and exit amiably. Unfortunately, he was having trouble with the credit card tape jamming up. Then the phone rang. Being the only clerk, he went around the corner to answer the phone. That took a while. Then he made a phone call about the obstinate machine he could not get to work.

I was looking for a wall to lean against.

Tears were going to fall down any minute, as much as I did not want them to. It was taking so long with all he was trying to do. By the time he was back at the counter and I was finally signing the receipt, tears were falling onto the paper, making wide wet circles, smearing the ink.

What was I to do? Not say anything? I looked him in the eye. I told him my firstborn child had just died. I told him this was Michael's phone and that I wanted to replace the battery so I could use the phone that was his. I told him thank you for his help. He was so sorry. I was so sorry. I hoped with all my heart I would be able to be gracious with all of the new experiences that were going to come my way.

Will I ever get used to saying, "Michael is dead?" Will the sound of his footsteps never go away? Would the sound of his voice always stay?

A haunting emptiness continued to torment us. Less mattered more and more. Little by little we were determining what mattered most. I felt the pull from the culture all around me to snap out of it, to not let the darkness envelop me. As if it were a choice. There seems to be great fear that if we engage with and fully enter into the heartache, we may not emerge out of it.

What if I didn't come out of the very dark place?

Do we construct facial facades instead?

Present an outward impression that appears to be religiously neat and orderly, obliquely confirming our conviction that God is good—in an attempt to conceal the unpleasant reality of the existential dishevelment within?

Would we let our life be defined by our tragedy? Would it become our identity? Would everything become futile to us, turning us into cynical, judgmental, annoying, going-through-the-motions-on-the-outside, seething-on-the-inside kind of people?

The alternative of not fully entering into the heartache seemed entirely unacceptable to me. I did not want to wear a mask and pretend everything was fine, although sometimes I did. Sometimes I still do.

I love my mask. I hate my mask. *"Love takes off masks that we fear we cannot live without and know that we cannot live within."* — *James Arthur Baldwin.* I do not want pity or pseudo love. Will I work harder at protecting myself from all of the things I don't want than courageously contending for the relationships I do want? What do I want? What do you want?

I don't want to live or die with a fake face or a pretend life.

I want a real one. Even if it means pain and suffering to get one.

Someone suggested to me I ought to be on antidepressants, saying they thought it would help me to not feel the pain. "Why would I not feel the pain?" I asked, wondering if the incredulity I felt on the inside was as obvious on the outside. "Why would you want to feel the pain if you don't have to?" they replied. As if taking medicine would take away the pain that Michael is dead. Not even God did that.

Would medicine somehow soothe sorrow in your soul? There is a cost to embracing soul pain, and often we would rather run fast and far away from it. We attempt to numb sorrow in all kinds of illogical ways. Soul pain is meant to be felt and explored. Is my self-protecting aversion to feeling pain so immense that I will refuse to let my soul struggle with our son's death in all of its enigma?

Maybe volcanic distress such as this has a way of inflaming more life. More passion. More sensitivity. More thoughtfulness. More internal capacity for what matters most. While there is much I do not understand yet, inexplicable sensations tell me there is something very important going on. I have no intention of camouflaging the pain.

In giving birth to Michael there were minor complications causing major pain throughout a long labor. My pain medicine then— was you. I was very aware of your gentle strength permeating the space beside me. Holding my hands. Holding my face. Looking me straight in the eye. Each blink of your eye flickered a story, bringing a remembering strength to me and the life within me.

Surrounded by each other, hand in hand, heart to heart, we

labored in love. Locking eyes, love bore the pain with a joy previously unknown. Could we comprehend the mystery of life forming inside my body as together we conceived and birthed our firstborn—and later his brother and sister—into the world? Can we conceive the mystery of death? Can our clasped hands of travailing-love-that-quells-pain hold them both—with the undaunted passion with which we have held each one of our newly born?

Is it possible to feel the pain yet not let it be the center of our life?

What is the center of our life?

How do we hold both joy and pain, awful and wonderful, comedy and tragedy, life and death? *"He is a sane man who can have tragedy in his heart and comedy in his head." —G. K. Chesterton.* Can we enlarge ourselves, internally, to embrace the expansiveness of each of these? Might that deepen the way we love each other?

In the midst of unrelenting upheaval intruding into each day, coffee remained an uncomplicated, intermittent reprieve. While you brew Folger's because it is what you especially enjoy, I decided to drink Starbuck's, not just on special occasions but every day, just because it is my favorite and I love it. Tempted to robotically dress in the same jeans and turtleneck, I determined to wear a different shirt every day.

And lipstick.

Lipstick makes you look more alive.

And it doesn't run when you cry.

Aftermath

TWO

✍

"The great thing, if one can, is to stop regarding all the unpleasant
things as interruptions of one's 'own' or 'real' life. The truth is of course
that what one calls the interruptions are precisely ones real life—
the life God is sending one, day by day."

—C. S. Lewis

IT WAS A FIERCELY MISERABLE MOMENT. There had been a lot of those lately. I can be back there in an instant. In a puddle of tears. Sitting against the wall on the floor in Michael's bedroom—which was a mess. Considering the mess we were in, it did not matter much.

You were sitting on his bed. We were contemplating Michael's things. I turned to you and said, "We desperately need help…"

Michael had been dead just over two months. Our marriage seemed suffocated and suppressed. Each of us was struggling with living. The oppressive characteristics of death surrounded us all. Having read and resonated with his books, I knew Dr. Larry Crabb was who I wanted to call. His secretary graciously gave us the names of two counselors.

We did not know either one, so we just picked one.

Tom's.

It is difficult to fully express how Tom Board related with us in ways we had never experienced before. Tom was not intimidated by our pain, tears, sorrow, sin, the chaos of our lives, or of death. In fact, he willingly walked with us into these treacherous places.

At one particularly difficult juncture, when faith was hard to find, *really* hard to find, Tom offered that I could borrow some of his. I have never forgotten. I am profoundly deep-as-the-sea grateful for Tom and to God for inviting me to so much more than I could have imagined life could be, and for pouring breath into me when I could barely breathe on my own. I am still a mess in many ways, but a more alive mess than ever before.

Do you remember our first conversation with Tom? He acknowledged it had not been very long since the accident. Obviously we were still raw and bleeding. Then he took the conversation in an interesting direction. He suggested we were being invited to enter into a place where, if we would go, could lead us to knowing God in ways we never had before. It would be hard. Uncomfortable. Take time.

Or. We could try to get back into life the best we could. Fill the pain with work, getting over it, and moving on. We would need to choose. One or the other.

With four people on such a painful journey living in the same house we were shivering in the intensity of it all. How do you love the people you love most in the whole world when you are each in so much distress? Hope wavered elusive. Tom offered us hope with a kind of weightiness that intrigued me. We were so thirsty for hope that was real.

The idea of invitation was an entirely new thought to me. It sounded more like a complex euphemism for a confrontation, an unwanted interruption. What could be appealing or enticing about this kind of invitation? What, exactly, would we be saying yes to?

There was a sense of grateful relief listening to the thoughtful language that Tom spoke and the way in which he spoke it. He was not pressing us toward life goes on, move on or get over it. There was no getting over it.

There was something vitally important happening that we were not entirely aware of. Tom recognized the battle that was going on within the deepest part of each of us, and he was willing to enter into it with us.

I remember a pastor telling us at Michael's funeral that, in general, people could handle sad for a couple of weeks and then they would be done with it. It did not fully register with me what he was saying at the time he said it. After a couple of weeks it started to sink in.

In the days and months just after Michael's funeral we were hurting in ways we could barely cope with, and I did not relate very well with people. Including you. From my perspective now, I would like to have related in ways I did not. Sorrow strangled us. Amidst the emotional debris whirling all around, it took considerable focused effort to recollect important parts of ourselves that we must not let be totally destroyed.

I was easily overwhelmed by the innocuous question "How are you?" Hearing it again and again and again and again was distressing. As usual, you were gracious. I knew people meant well and that it was mostly a passive form of greeting. I began to respond with what I wish they would say instead. "It is good to see you." I was miserable. Confused and consumed by fear and grief. I became more miserable when anyone tried to cheer me up. I knew people did not know what to do with me. I did not know what to do with me either. I believed them when they said they wanted to help. Just tell them what to do, they offered, and they would do anything. "Call anytime," they always said.

I do not want to call anyone. I do not know what to tell them.

We were entirely caught off guard by how emotionally difficult it became to go to church. There was a lot of perky at church. Perky skits. Music. Words. People. Much more perky than either of us could manage. Everywhere I went outside the consolatory enclosure of our home, people were laughing. Acting so normal.

I could hardly talk. They could hardly be quiet. Forever asking, "How are you?"

Life had every appearance of moving on, for others. It seemed important to them that I understand that. They told me often, "Life goes on. So should you." What does that mean, I wonder. "You have to live your life." "You have your memories." "You still have two children." "God must have needed Michael more." "Things could be worse."

They do not know … how burningly aware I am that things could be worse and how it frightens me.

"Find closure and be happy." Find closure and be happy?

"Did you know, in biblical times, people were given seven days to mourn their dead?"

I have no doubts I too have said many foolish things. I shudder to think.

In the holy-overwhelming-God-given-kairos-interruption, life does not just go on.

I am intensely wondering—what does it mean to live your life? How is life defined, and by whom? What does dead feel like? I am sure I feel more dead than alive. I am stuck in this divergent place and can hardly move.

The composition of the texture of our relationships—the manner in which the threads of our lives were being woven with many of our friends—was becoming strikingly rearranged. We were not becoming more integrated and whole but more torn apart and isolated. Things were starting to fray and unravel. Mostly me.

I had no idea how to navigate this disheartening place.

We were extremely touched when many people from near and far expressed great kindness to us following the accident. Now, our closest relationships were feeling stress fractures as the reality of it all began to sink in. It was disconcerting to me that relationships were becoming difficult and full of strife. We could not go back to their world, and they were unable to enter into ours. We were missing each other, not meaningfully meeting each other. You and I would not be able to rearrange ourselves to what used to be. We would have to face the screaming internal struggles in our souls.

Not only was there a very big sorrow in Michael dying, there were so many little sorrows that kept piling up. It seemed crushingly clear that many of our relationships were not going to survive the bursting inward collapse from the recent implosion in general. Or our gutted deconstructed selves in particular.

It seemed just as clear I had a lot yet to learn about love that is alive and what it means to die to your self.

The sound of the phone ringing continued to put me on edge and made my heart race. A friend was calling to tell me she had been praying for God to take away all the pain of Michael's death because she could not handle it. And that God did.

It was another leaning-against-the-wall-and-sliding-to-the-floor moment.

Her pain so easily, so quickly taken away. Too, she thought I should know that people were tired of trying to help us and were giving up, but she felt like God would not let her give up on me. Sincerely wanting to help, she continued, "I don't know what to do with you. Just tell me what to do. You are dealing with this so differently than most of us would."

I had so many thoughts. I kept them to myself.

More ringing. More racing. A friend was calling to tell me she just wants to help and thinks it would help for me to know what she has been hearing. I have hurt a lot of people's feelings. She thought I should know that I am being very difficult. Why didn't I want to let them take care of us? Why wouldn't we let people in on our grief? Why do I get upset when people ask how are you—they are just being nice.

More ringing. More racing. A friend is calling to tell me she needs to know that I am fine and wants to hear me say it. She can't imagine this happening to her. I am aware what she wants the most is to hear me say I am fine. I tell her I am not so fine. I tell her I am pretty much a mess. I tell her I too hope this never happens to her. Another sad, awkward goodbye.

More ringing. More racing. A friend is calling to ask me if I would like to go walking with her. She is not particularly fond of dogs, but she would not mind at all if I brought mine. I liked my friend just being and breathing beside me in comfortable quiet.

The relational texture of the most outer layer of me feels stingingly abrasive. Coarse and gritty, like sandpapery asphalt shingles. Further in, I was shutting down and closing up. I do not know how to make my way through relationships. I would rather be like leather. Flexible. Strong. Beautiful. Inviting. Even if worn and weathered.

What does it mean to love each other in this place?

I hoped with all my heart someday I would be able to relate differently. Part of me wanted to engage with people. Part of me just wanted to be left alone. We seemed to be stuck in demanding places personally and were relating in demanding ways collectively. I felt so much pressure. I knew I was not coming through for people like they hoped I would. They were not coming through for me in ways I hoped they would either. *"We are too quick to resent and feel what we suffer from others, but fail to consider how much others suffer from us."* —*Thomas à Kempis.*

Again and again I found myself wondering what it really means to die to self.

Exhausted from squirming in uncomfortable places, the distance between our friends and us grew.

A pastor had a challenge for us. "Why won't you leave some room for people who are clueless? They have something, even if it is just friendship and support, to offer you. You should share with us what you are learning through this."

Maybe I am the one who is clueless. Michael's death is not some sort of vicarious lesson. Life seems to be pressing in on me from every side, and I am out of room. I feel like a flickering friend whose unsteady flame does not want to go out but is going out anyway, and I feel awful that others are experiencing us as being difficult. I am aware we are making people uncomfortable.

I would evaporate if I could.

How I wish it would rain. Rain forever.

I love the rain. Especially when it thunders. Remember when we used to walk in the rain? I love walking in the rain, without an umbrella, looking up into the stormy sky. Feeling every single uninhibited drop of wetness soak into me. I love walking in the rain, with an umbrella, tucked in all cozy underneath. Listening to the music the moisture makes as it falls on the fabric. Watching how the earth absorbs the nourishing, life-giving gift.

Mostly, I love walking to the rhythm of the rain with you. Instinctively we lock arms. Synchronize our footsteps. Even the tempo of our heart-to-heart words falls into a harmonious cadence with the regular, repeated pattern of the falling water. Sometimes we jump in puddles—splashing joy all over each other.

I fell in love with you ... walking and splashing joy in the rain.

How much rain would it take to wash away this mess, to germinate shriveled seeds of dormant hope inside? But I'm still here. Uncooperative. Unpredictable. Unmanageable. Uncontrollable. A great big mess.

No wonder people say, "I don't know what to do with you."

I will still look people in the eye.

Even if mine are all wet.

You don't have to look in anyone's eyes when you send an email. You can say anything you want to, any way you want to, then click send and not be anywhere near when they read your words. Attached to a story called "Satan's Tools for Sale," describing the most expensive one being discouragement, was a note. "You have isolated yourselves from the church community for far too long and it must come to an end." Even if they would have said it to us in person, these words did not have the well-intentioned quality of encouragement. You were generous. You said, "They are just trying." I realized then that I am just trying, too. I am trying as hard as I can, and it is not working out very well.

Maybe dying to yourself and really truly loving people has not much to do with "trying."

I do not want you or Tyler or Megan to ever be in the place where what you say is, "She's just trying." I want so much more for each of you. I am going to think really hard about what it means to give it to you. What it really means to be with you, to love you with the kind of energy and passion that God loves you, no matter how much I am hurting inside of myself.

It seemed the pastor who had cautioned us about the low degree to which most people can deal with sadness knew what he was talking about. After trying to help and not knowing what to do with us or our indelible sadness, most people reluctantly gave up. We were heartbroken over our extreme loss and unable to receive much of the help they wanted to give. There is a tendency to want to fix something, to do something pragmatic that would make both us and them feel better relatively quickly. To get us to come back into life as it was before, as the people they used to know.

We are not the same people as we were. How could we be? There is no going back. I think I thought my faith was a lot stronger than it is proving to actually be. Things that used to seem so important don't seem so important anymore.

It is a daunting thing to feel and seriously wrestle with intense pain deep within your soul, intense questions regarding everything you thought you believed about God. Many of us go to great extent in trying to evade soul pain, as if that would be the most noble choice. We focus instead on being busy. We are very busy, proud people, and we desperately want to be happy people, not sad. Philosophers and theologians of old would define happy much differently than we do today.

Most of us are scared to death of death. We are taught that grief has five stages. Our culture seems to insist on defining clear-cut expectations and outcomes, as if grief and sorrow are problems to be solved through mastering certain techniques.

In giving guidelines on how to minimize grief and sorrow there is an emphasis put on either overcoming it or making something good come out of it. I just read an article suggesting we medicalize grieving and characterize it as a disorder.

That is one of the most grievous things I have ever read.

What happens to a person, a culture, a world—that does not, will not, grieve or lament?

Insisting on lessening the intensity of experiencing sorrow to the lowest degree possible entirely misses accepting and absorbing the enormous gift that sorrow offers to us in its unmitigated, essential nature.

Pain and heartache are indescribable to someone who has never been inside of them. There was absolutely nothing anyone could do to make us feel better. That was the wrong battle, and we intuitively knew it deep within.

I want to move in a direction that takes my soul to absorb more of what matters most. What is it that matters most? Do I believe the Gospel is true? Strategies, assumptions, agendas, logical formulas all fall away when staring death straight in the face. What we really believe to be true about God is confronted at the most essential level. Do I *really* believe things are not entirely as they seem, that God *is* real? Do you?

Tom's gentle voice remains in my head. And his generous words. There is something intrinsically meaningful in knowing God, in deeper ways, in this place. There are searing, sacred moments that change us forever. Moments that send us on a journey we could never have imagined.

We decided to accept the invitation. It was to be unlike any invitation I have ever known. No handwritten calligraphy. No ivory silk luxe paper. No personalized wax seal. I would not have recognized it as an Invitation of the Most Precious Kind were it not for, in God's unleashed mercy, the spiritual direction of Tom.

When the circumstances of life became more than we could bear, he kept the vision of the invitation open. Engaging in conversations with us that were too threatening for anyone else we knew, he entered into the seemingly unending chaos of both life and death that had unexpectedly become the struggling reality of our life.

Aftermath

THREE

༄

*"We will not encounter Christ as our best friend, as the source
of all true goodness, as the One who provides the sweetest pleasure
to our souls, until we abandon ourselves to Him. And full
abandonment, real trust, rarely happens until we meet God in the
midst of shattered dreams, until in our brokenness we see in Him
the only and overflowingly sufficient answer to our soul's deepest cry."*
—Dr. Larry Crabb, *Shattered Dreams*

B EING IN A CONTINUED STATE OF debilitating unsettledness forces you to face the unsettledness. I found
it to be an unceasing, drawn-out disturbance on the
inside and the outside of me. My fear was moving me toward God. My
fear was moving me away from God.

I think my fear was smothering you.

I was carelessly unaware of how intensely determined I was to
manage life, attempting to manipulate God in such a way that things
would be well, as I defined well, for me and for our family. Presently,
things are not well at all.

Our dreams have been totally shattered. Suddenly. Violently.
Broken into pieces. I have been broken into pieces. It is incredibly hard
for me to find the words to describe the depth of trouble I found myself
in. I felt like prayer was all I had, but I had no idea how to pray. Not to
mention I was fiercely mad at God. I did not believe He would listen
to me.

There was something strong in me yet, although you may not see it if you looked at the outside of me. Michael dying will not be merely a speed bump along the way we call life. I will not give into resignation and submit calmly to the death of my child. Nor will I give up and attempt to live with an absence of passion for life.

The only way I know how to do both is to stay in this disturbing place of unsettling circumstances. Where will it take me? What if I never make my way out? Worse, what if I miss out on the opportunity to grow deeper in vital ways that are indispensable to the discovery of real life, unless I am willing to enter into the darkness?

Mixed feelings of wonder, dread, and reverential fear whirl all around and in me. There must be something of significant importance here to have been given such an occasion for such an invitation.

An intense crisis in my faith had begun to emerge in ways I had never known before. Tom asked me one day, "Have you been so hurt by God that you don't really want to know Him?"

I had imagined a persona of God who would be quick to help me in ways I would consider to be helpful. But such help never came. Maybe real help can only come from real God. Can I tell the difference between what is real and what isn't? Maybe God is up to something incredible, the most-real-beautiful, and I am all wrapped up tight in illusions and assumptions.

I meant it when I said I do not want a pretend life. How is it then I would settle for an imagined persona of God? God is who He is. Who is He? He is not defined by me.

I must give up my artificially induced image of Him if I want to know the true Him. Why does that feel scary to me? What is the incessant fear that keeps getting in the way?

I said yes to the invitation, and I meant it. In deciding to say yes, I thought hard about if I even believed God existed or not. What I believe about Him had never been so tested or tempted. I am saying yes to the invitation. Which means I am saying yes to Him.

It was agitating to uncover what I had, rather passively, come to believe about God. Nothing about Him feels lethargic anymore. It feels like we are in a sweeping struggle. The audacious thought of it—

struggling with God. It is of some small comfort to know that other troubled souls have struggled with God too.

The sheer volume of chaos saturating our lives during this time was intense and threatened to rob all courage and strength. How do we live rattled around in the ambivalence that living in such a chaotic place brings? Slog through the best we can?

I was aware of feeling broken, in the sense of considerable pain. I was becoming more cognizant of how unbroken I was in regard to the reality of the ways in which I was relating out of that pain, making me the one who was causing considerable pain to you and to others.

This became especially poignant to me on the day I came to see that the truculent words my friend had said to me were essentially the same words I had communicated to Tyler. "I don't know what to do with you."

Struggling with God. Struggling with Tyler. Struggling with myself. I am filled with disgust and despair over the bruising impact I am having on our son. Sometimes in the squeezing pain and confusion within relationships, I just do not know what to do or say. The words we choose to speak and the energy with which we speak them have incalculable impact on the soul of another. How wrong of me to be so unreflecting, so unwary, with such a treasure.

It had not been long since Michael's funeral when we met with Tyler's probation officer. I was anxious and apprehensive. Quiet and bracingly calm, you were strong like a rod. Rods are used in structures to tie, hold, and bind supporting members together so that they do not sway, rack, or shift. In all that pulling tension you tied yourself to me, keeping both of us upright and together throughout the invasive questions about our marriage, our personal relationships, what our house looked like. I was incredulous that it might matter what our house looked like. Michael's recent death never came up.

An especially eerie question, "Do you want to keep Tyler? You could give him up." The perfunctory tone with which she spoke such grave words made me wonder if I had misunderstood. I was stunned and did not know if my heart could handle any more of this type of violent turbulence. What does she mean, give him up? Why did she ask us this? Did we say something to make her think we don't want him? Does he think we don't want him? Does he not want us? It was more than ridiculous to think we would "give him up" over some foolish sophomoric rebellion.

I looked her in the eye. "No, we do not want to give him up. Why would we do that? He is our son. He is so loved. And so wanted."

"I don't know what to do with you" kept reverberating throughout my being, making me feel nauseous. I was coming to realize not only had that been my attitude toward Tyler, but God too.

More and more sorrows.

Maybe this is how You see me, God, in my own selfish rebellion. Maybe You are not as angry as I think. Maybe Your anger is different than mine in some ways. Maybe You cry too. Tears of pain over the way I relate to You. How I dismiss You. Avoid You. Look right at You but don't really see You. You would never say, "I don't know what to do with you." You would say, "Will you see how much I love you?" You gave Your life to say, "No. I do not want to give her up. She is so loved. And so wanted."

Would I give my life to say that? What would I give my life for? It is becoming urgently necessary to clarify how it is that life is defined in order to live.

Through many forming conversations with Tom, I came face-to-face with the unpleasant discovery of how insistent I had become in my effort to control circumstances and people in an attempt to get life to work the way I wanted it to. I let fear manage me in troublesome ways, and I used fear to justify my controlling demeanor. Justifying the ways I relationally hurt you and others while wriggling in fearful, painful places is awful-ugly and must have had a discouraging impact on you.

I had no logical comprehension of how intensely I wanted life to be safe and secure. For our children not to die. For things to go well for them. For God to bless them. I lost realistic conception of how much I wanted life to be on my terms, demanding God give it to me. My plan. My timetable. My way, as if I could make it all safe.

I had so many hopes and dreams regarding our children, and us. I have been all crooked in clamoring for their story to be one I would choreograph to be good. As if I could humanly calculate what can only be the affairs of God for a soul. How is it that I came to such a choking place? How had I come to regard them, or you, as mine to have?

"*There might be things more terrible even than losing someone you love by death.*" —*C. S. Lewis.* I curled up one afternoon on the quarter-sawn oak mission-style sofa that I had carried home from the thrift store on the top of our little car so many years ago. Do you remember when we brought it into the house? I bet in your head you were thinking, what has she dragged home this time, but you were always affable regarding my enthusiasm for refinishing, repurposing, and remaking old, interesting things.

At the time, the children were very young. You laid down on the sofa to test out the ancient springs, and all three of them piled horizontally—one on top of the other—on top of you. All stacked up and giggling. That sofa, stuffed with so many stories, is one of my favorite things.

It was autumn. My favorite season. I was about to read *The Great Divorce* written by C. S. Lewis, one of my favorite authors. I had no idea the wringing afternoon I was in for.

The Great Divorce, written in 1946, is an allegory; a story interpreted to reveal a hidden meaning. The divorce Lewis refers to is between Heaven and Hell. The story takes place on a bus that is traveling between the two. It is a book of conversations. Ghosts have been released from Hell to visit Heaven, where redeemed spirits try to persuade them into staying. In essence, it is a meditation upon good and evil.

I was thoroughly enjoying the book. I am always enthralled by Lewis's gift of depth and insight into important spiritual truths and the language he uses to communicate them. I actually chuckled at the story of Robert and his Ghost wife. Feelings of affection for and casual connection with the characters drew me deeper and deeper into the hiddenness of the intricate vanities being presented. At the same time I was becoming squirmy with the idea that I too may be more ghost, less solid, than I realized. Then I read the next conversational story.

A Bright Spirit named Reginald is meeting with a woman's Ghost named Pam. The Ghost is looking for her son named Michael. She was demanding to see him. The Bright Spirit attempts to explain to her that she needs to be "thickened up a bit" before that will ever happen.

"Oh, you mean religion and all that sort of thing? I'll do whatever's necessary. What do you want me to do? Come on. The sooner I begin it, the sooner they'll let me see my boy. I'm quite ready."

"But, Pam, do think! Don't you see you are not beginning at all as long as you are in that state of mind? You're treating God only as a means to Michael. But the whole thickening treatment consists in learning to want God for His own sake."

"You wouldn't talk like that if you were a mother."

"You mean, if I were only a mother. But there is no such thing as being only a mother. You exist as Michael's mother only because you first exist as God's creature. That relation is older and closer. No, listen, Pam! He also loves. He also has suffered. He also has waited a long time."

As the conversation goes on the Spirit tries to explain to the ghost mother how what she thought was love was a strangling, selfish kind of love, not real love. She had mistaken natural love for eternal love.

Who would dare go to a miserable mother whose child was dead and challenge her like that? Tell her that she could not fully love her son until she loved God first? That in her misery, her loneliness, something else might start to grow?

The ghost mother was highly offended. She did not think that she had made her child a false god. She was not willing to either accept that she loved Michael more than she loved God or that there was anything wrong with that if, indeed, she had.

She began to compare herself with other mothers and children who were not as perfectly behaved as she and her children were. They deserved this kind of horrid treatment, but certainly she did not. No one's sorrow could be as deep as hers. Not even the sufferings belonging to her husband or her daughter.

I am all tied up in knots. Or is it that I am completely untied? Chuckles have turned to tears. I get a box of tissues. I breathe some autumn air. I snuggle deeper into the comforting, storied sofa. I keep reading.

"I don't believe in a God who keeps mother and son apart. I believe in a God of love. No one had a right to come between me and my son. Not even God. Tell Him that to His face. I want my boy and I mean to have him. He is mine, do you understand? Mine, mine, mine, for ever and ever."

"He will be, Pam. Everything will be yours. God Himself will be yours. But not that way."

Did he have to use the name Michael? That made the story all the more particular to me. I pinch myself, wanting to feel something solid. Internally I am not feeling solid at all. I become agonizingly aware that I am part ghost. Ghost mother. Ghost wife. Ghost period.

The story of Reginald, Pam, and Michael had just become very personal and perfectly clear. I was coming to realize in ways I never had before how preeminently attached I have become to you and our children. How insistent my desire is for life to go the way I wish it would. As if life would be managed, manipulated, and obedient to me.

How is it that a mother's love, seemingly so beautiful, could be so distortedly transposed into an entirely different—dissonant—key, becoming not at all like eternal love that originated with God?

I think Pam's way has been my way too. My love has been strangling and selfish, and I did not even see it. Do I really want God for His own sake or as a means to Michael?

What would it mean if I were to abandon myself to You, God? I can't even seem to find You. You would not abandon us, would You? You also have loved. You also have suffered. You also have waited a long time. I think eternal love has everything to do with what You were going through in Gethsemane right before You offered Yourself as our sacrifice. What if I die never having loved the people I love the most with love that is eternal? What would it mean to love You with love that is eternal?

Michael is dead. Tyler is struggling. I see Megan's sorrows. And yours. I am grieving for each of you in different ways. I walk gingerly through the holy shards, slivers, and splinters of our broken lives, hoping not to break anything more. Wondering if the searing cry of my soul could be any deeper.

Maybe things are not as they seem. Maybe He is deeper still. Still with us. Always seeing. Always inviting. Did I think that our dreams should not be shattered? That we should not be shattered? How did what I thought was an honest, wholesome love come to be revealed as such a contracting, pulled-tight, protecting, suffocating kind of thing? This must have impacted you and our children in stifling ways. Are there things that could be more terrible than losing someone we love by death?

Like Pam, I need to be thickened up a bit. I am a fertile ground of misery right now.

Perhaps something alive might grow in the generative potential of this incisive place.

Aftermath

FOUR

∾

*"But it is important too not to miss the God-content in the darkness.
An offer of freedom from ourselves, for a God who fills. To trust—that
God is present in this—can turn the pain, where there has to be pain,
from death-throes into the pangs of birth."*

—Iain Matthews, *The Impact of God*

AN INTERNAL URGENCY INTENSIFIED WITHIN ME to determine the true definition of life. Experiencing the reality of death was helping me to see more clearly the reality of life. I was starting to understand how I had been gripping, with fists clenched tight, definitions of life that were not really true. The anguish of death is distinctly less dim than before Michael died. Life and death are substantial words sometimes used in casual ways, but clearly they are not casual concepts. Staring death in the face confronts you in ways only death can.

My quest for real life was to become an all-out internal battle, the battle of my life. It felt like life or death because it was. *"You never know how much you really believe anything until its truth or falsehood becomes a matter of life and death to you." —C. S. Lewis.* There is something that feels sacred about this battle. How could anything be stronger than death?

Death has a distinct way of challenging anything taken for granted and false appearances, but those things were not to be dispelled easily. It would take time for them to disperse and radically collapse.

It is taking a long time for me to see The Invitation for what it truly is.

This battle plunged me straight into the deep end of darkness. I had no idea how dark dark could be. There were dreadful things I discovered about myself in the forever long, dark night. Things I did not like. I was not sure what to do with them. Malevolent anxiety and uncertainty gripped me as if they were an insoluble adhesive, leaving me petrified, that I would never be separated from them.

I was uncertain how to stay in this sunless, moonless, starless, other-less place, but I could see no way out. I could only see dark despair. There was no sense of defined space. Only endless, unrelenting darkness.

What if, in its unyielding determination, it swallows me whole, and I find that I am not just in it but am it?

The reality of the battle is much bigger and more intense than I could have imagined, but in my frenetic fury I am ready for a fight. A crazy, crying, angry mother. You do not want to mess with me.

But life has messed with me.

I am being crushed under the hostile weight of all that is going on—but the pulling of the gravitational force of the burden of sorrow within provokes me toward experiencing the full force of the grief. The anger. The ambivalence. I have no control over death, which has ripped my heart out—like it could be had just for the taking. There are times I feel like giving up and giving in. God remains invisible. I am coming to my wit's end. Will I find there is more solidity to me than wits?

Am I going to leave my heart where death left it—for dead? Am I going to let my anger take—whatever is left of me—wherever it wants to go? So-called strategies for coping are irrelevant in this random, difficult-to-understand, desperate place.

Will it ever, ever, ever be well with my soul? What would that mean exactly?

My mentally exhausted, anxious, and angry self wants to take the whatever-is-left-of-me to the garage. Around this time I happened to discover a newly released book written by Dr. Armand M. Nicholi, Jr. titled *The Question of God: C. S. Lewis and Sigmund Freud Debate God, Love, Sex, and the Meaning of Life.*

I stayed up night after night reading and contemplating their individual stories of struggling with God and with death. As a fellow human being I could relate to each of them in different ways. Their similar struggles and contrasting choices inspired me to stay engaged with my own.

Ultimately I came to the conclusion I did not want to die seething in anger, refusing to be refused, and demanding to have my own insistent, peremptory way in the very end.

I did not let myself take myself to the garage.

Whoever wrote that silly email message was wrong. Satan has a much more disturbing weapon in his tool bag than discouragement, that being death. Not to entirely dismiss him, but there is something very much bigger going on than his fire sale. For God's great weapon is also death. We can try to ignore death.

Death will not be ignored.

Death remains a mystery in many ways. Death raises a lot of questions. Death itself is a question.

I am seeing more and more profoundly the profundity of the question.

Death can only destroy what is destructible. What is the indestructible that death cannot ever destroy? What was it that kept You from being internally destroyed that night in Gethsemane? What compelled You to die on the cross? What is love that is eternal?

Maybe the only way to know You in this place is in this place.

After considerable difficulty my eyes and my heart began adjusting to see from a different perspective. Can anything illuminating come out of dark? One of the significant things that being in the dark brought to light was an emerging, slow work of transformation regarding the definition of life. The dark gradually thickens you, strengthens and solidifies integral parts of you, causing growth in ways only dark can. This is not only a place of intense grief—but a rupturing of life as I have known it, challenging how and what I think and reshaping how I see living and dying and loving. Something indestructible is growing in me, in the dark. I must not run away from the difficulty of it.

Synthetic fabrications—assumptions—and false pretenses—illusions—were being revealed for what they really are. Empty. Without weight. Arrogant. Unable to bring fulfilled meaning to completion.

Block by block, over most of my life, I had been building misleading mental images of a happy and blessed life, unconsciously guarding my mirages tenaciously.

It seems my definition of sin has been much too small.

There was a tremendous degree of detaching necessary in confronting the intensity of my desire to personally control my own circumstances and provide for myself. The way I have been defining life is being profoundly shifted.

The dark is isolating and desolately lonely. So lonely. The pervading tone is bleakly unadorned and perturbing, but I began to be less intimidated. The dark woke me up in startling ways. Bitterness and resentment began to fade. I began to embrace the darkness and my suffering. I cannot, nor do I any longer want to, escape from this juncture of persistent collisions but rather enter into it with all of my being.

It is a core-to-core confrontation regarding life and death and love, surprisingly arousing hope that I thought was gone forever.

A profound sense of more began to unfold. I have been settling for less.

I will weep until I see the more. The more that transcends the pain.

The darkness has given me increased perspective and an emerging clarity about God that I have not been aware of before. The darkness took me deeper into emptiness but also deeper into irrevocable fullness. The darkness revealed frightening ugliness but unveiled inspiring beauty.

I sensed both a joining and a separating. I am less certain about the truth of some things, but I am more certain about the truth of some things. I am becoming more accepting of complexity and mystery.

Through this darkness lasting over a period of years, I began to discover that I can live from my soul more than from my self.

Just because I thought God was invisible doesn't mean He wasn't there.

You are always there, aren't you, God?

Right here.

Even in the dark.

The dark, deep place—where You are the only one who could reach—this dark, deep place in me.

I see now how indelibly attached, stuck-like-glue, to you and our children I am. I had never been so happy as when you and I fell in love. Got married. Brought three children into the world.

Do you know how madly in love with you I am?

We were a world. Our own little kingdom of stories and songs and favorites. Books. Colors. Music. Meals. Dogs. Ice cream. Blankets. Pillows. Parks. People. Spaces. Shared experiences. You and our children have been the most important living beings in the universe to me.

"I can't believe I get you."

You have been the primary source of immeasurable pleasure and extreme joy in my life.

You have been "life" to me in many ways, as I have insisted life be on my terms and according to my definition. A self-centered life more than an eternal-loving-centered life. I am Michael's mother from *The Great Divorce*.

Does trying to make you my source of life turn my love for you into a strangling, suffocating sort of thing that does not honorably reveal life or love at all? Only ruins the legitimate beauty of the ecstatic joy and delight I find in you?

Unsticking myself from you would be like dismembering a vital part of me.

My exorbitant delight became my outrageous tragedy.

Who, besides Reginald, would sit and chat with a miserable mother whose child was dead and challenge her theology of life and death and love?

Tom would.

It is disconcerting to realize what I wanted most was for God to cooperate with me in keeping you and our children safe from harm and for our lives to go relatively well, according to my definition. I pretty much interpreted the meaning of the universe to be me, and you, and us, more than relational communion with God—who gives meaning and is the ultimate meaning of the universe.

I wonder what it is like for You, to love us so much that You sacrificed Your life to be with us, and we could be with You. To love us and we could love You. Enjoy us and we could enjoy You. But being with You, loving You, and enjoying You was not what we wanted most. What we wanted most was for You to cooperate with us in getting whatever else it is—family—health—career—enough money—all kinds of happy-blessing-things—that we want so much more. That must be intensely painful for You. You are well acquainted with relational pain, aren't You?

With poetic vision, Tom listened with an unusual curiosity to my messy, tearful stories. He perceptively heard more than just my words. Believing there is purpose and meaning in the darkness and in that place is where God does some of His deepest work, Tom did not retreat from the confusion as I writhed in it. With unwavering strength and vision he spoke into the chaos, touching my soul, where the battle raged the most ferociously between selfishness and holiness.

He did not scold or shame me. Caught up in the larger story of God, he stayed with me. Believing God to be more powerful than the chaos of darkness, Tom spoke into the darkness words of life. Life entered where it seemed there was only death.

I kept forgetting.

Tom kept remembering.

With unshakable patience he reminded me of who God is. A relational community of three persons. Father. Son. Spirit. Their way of relating defines love, and they invite us into their relationship of love.

Reminding me that my soul is fundamentally relational. The pain I am feeling could open my soul to experience my deepest desire—which is God. Suffering, sorrow, loneliness, darkness, and pain are indescribable gifts that lead me to relate with God in profound ways. You are a gift in how you provoke me to know God in deeply beautiful ways I would never have known without knowing you.

Reminding me that my deepest battle is not about Michael dying, or Tyler or Megan or you, but the restoration of my soul—

to know and enjoy God as my deepest passion, not as a means to anything else.

Reminding me that things are not as they seem. We are part of a much larger story, an eternal love story.

Reminding me that I wanted real and I have been invited to real.

Reminding me that God wants to relate to me, and my soul wants to believe, but I often rebel and resist. I really do desire to know God and reveal something beautiful of Him in the way I relate with others.

Tom never gave up on God. Awakening my longing and thirst for God, Tom never gave up on me either.

The definition of real life seems so complicated but so simple. So easy but so hard. We have been invited to real. God is real. He defines life. He brings meaning to life. He is life. He is the real meaning of life. He invites us to life in and with Him.

God has known so much pain. He knows intimately what it is like to be in pain over relationships. Maybe at some level we can relate to Him in this place. Shared moments of both joy and sorrow.

Because He poured out His life for us, we can pour out our life for others. Because He pours life into us, we can pour life into others.

While surrounded by dark, I came to see there really is something alive in me. I can die to my self and as I do, I can live and love more from my soul than my self.

I still cry. *"There is a sadness in tears. They are not the mark of weakness, but of power. They speak more eloquently than ten thousand tongues. They are messengers of overwhelming grief and unspeakable love."* —Washington Irving. No longer the stinging, angry tears that come from a place of rage, but holy and sacred tears that come from a place of intense enrapture.

To think—You request the pleasure of our company. You invite us into Your Three-in-One relational community. It is hard for me to fathom such mystery. You invite us into holy, fiercely beautiful relationship. You seek us with all of Your heart. You long for us to find You, eternal love and life.

Building

ONE
ৎ৶

"It is in dialogue with pain that many beautiful things acquire their value. Acquaintance with grief turns out to be one of the more unusual prerequisites of architectural appreciation. We might, quite aside from all other requirements, need to be a little sad before buildings can properly touch us."

—Alain de Botton

DIALOGUE WITH PAIN CAME TO BE a normal part of everyday life and conversation between you and me. It might accost us when we least expected it, sparking intense conversation. It might whisper loud in the dark quiet. Naked and unashamed took on new levels of relational meaning. Words might be necessary, or not, in the communion of sharing intimate thoughts and feelings about what was going on inside of us. Struggle continues in each of us at varying degrees.

We see things we did not see before severe tragedy came to us. Acquaintance with grave grief brought with it never-before-explored dimensions, perspectives, and relational textures, enabling us to touch and be touched in ways untouchable before.

Amidst the stormy stress, you—my faithful friend, my husband, my Architect—did what you do. Create ordered beauty out of chaos, metaphoric images out of light and shadow, bricks and wood. You designed a house. For us. I did not want to build a house. I loved the 1940s charming Cape Cod on the quaint, tree-lined street. We had nested in deep. Our handprints and footprints were woven in and out and all over that place.

We had recently taken a sledgehammer to the ugly square bathtub and worn-out red tile; the bathroom we just remodeled was the most striking bathroom I had ever seen. I was particularly fond of the antique compass paper on the ceiling—it was worth the neck ache I had for a week after pasting it up there.

I loved the stories in the walls. And the one on the dining room ceiling. You and Michael had painted a work of art for the light fixture to center itself in over the table. Its geometrical shape shimmered in the light of evening with an enchanting kind of twinkle, teasing me to recall the comedic saga of how the two of you went about creating this fine masterpiece. Everywhere I look, a story looks right back at me. I do not want to build a new one. I want this one.

Maybe part of us wanted to escape being surrounded by the familiar walls of stories and closely associated family footings. Maybe we would never let ourselves leave, mournfully clinging to our memories and shared history of where the children had grown up. We must not run away in wailing escape or graspingly never leave in a vain attempt for consolation that will never come from clinging and grasping to things this way.

It is not uncommon for people to become sentimentally attached to their homes and even name them. This happens in cultures all around the world. Our homes shelter us physically, but they seem to offer more than that. As life unfolds within and around us our homes take on a distinct character of their own, almost like they are part of the family. Our homes, the materials they are constructed of, and the furnishings in them trigger memories and stories. "*A man travels the world over in search of what he needs, and returns home to find it." —George Moore.* I remember a pizza delivery boy standing in the entrance of the Cape Cod one night as he pointed at this quote on the wall and said, "I have to disagree with that." I was curious where and who he called home, what he was searching for, what he thought he needed.

I like to hear stories of what people remember about the house they grew up in. The people they lived with. Favorite rooms. Colors. Furniture. Floors. Nooks and crannies. Distinct smells. What the dishes were like. Best-loved blankets. Sources of light. Hiding places and pets. Pianos, violins, saxophones, drums, clarinets, old radios, and record players—the music that was played throughout a life.

Gardens, barns, climbing trees, eccentric neighbors. A favorite heat register or radiator to curl up and read a book with. A perfectly positioned window to watch and wonder what was going on outside from the perspective of being inside. The conversations and relationships that left lasting marks of beauty, shame, fear, joy on a life.

Most people remember the first home they moved into all on their own. Where they lived when they first got married. Brought home their first baby. The multilayered spatial emptiness endured when death comes to one of the two-become-one-flesh-until-death-do-us-part, leaving the other to bury their beloved.

Remember the Sheep House?

Megan was just turning one year old when we moved into the Sheep House. She was just turning seven when we moved out. In the in between she grew indelibly attached. That house made a mark on her little-girl life that is not easily removed. All three of our children were unusually emotional over that house. Is it the house or is it what happened in and around the house? I think it is both. She will tell you anything you want to know about that house. Just ask her. She remembers everything.

We dubbed it the Sheep House because at one time it was part of a farm with sheep. It was built in 1890 for two thousand dollars. The owner had moved to the area to become law partners with William Jennings Bryan. His brother, Charles Dawes, was vice president of the

United States under Calvin Coolidge. This property is no longer farm country but part of a historic district in the middle of the city.

Megan considered her bedroom a sacred space. It had a glass-handled door with a transom window across the top that could be opened in order to circulate air. It had two windows that were taller than she was and a charming four-poster bed that we dragged home from the thrift store and painted slate blue. It had lots of bookshelves with lots of books. She could see the stars out of the tall windows as she fell asleep at night.

We had sold the house and were about to move out when I discovered Megan in the bathroom tearing a piece of wallpaper off the wall. I knelt down and asked her about what she was doing. With a sad, small voice she said, "I don't ever want to forget what it looks like."

Then she showed me her writings.

She had been all around the two-story house counting doors, closets, windows, radiators, lightbulbs, ceiling fans, shelves, sinks, cupboards, and electrical outlets. She wrote it all down. She wrote about the pantry, the kitchen, the swing on the front porch, the patio and fireplace in the backyard that you built for us, out of one-hundred-year-old pavers, to roast marshmallows in.

We sat together on the bathroom floor remembering her whole life. I found extra wallpaper, and we patched the tear. She cut samples to save along with her writing.

I have saved it all.

It was when we moved into the Sheep House that we established "Super Friday Family Fun Night." It usually began Friday afternoon when mom and children might trek to the thrift stores. You never know what you might discover. Books and games that were like brand new. Only better. Old computers, irons, mixers, toasters, clocks, tape recorders, coffeepots. Any small appliance that could be taken apart to try to figure out how it worked. Taking things apart also provided a great collection of all sorts of bits and parts to put together on your own, creating new inventions. Every once in a while a great old piece of furniture, like a tall four-poster bed. A desk. A dresser. An antique quarter-sawn oak mission-style sofa for thirty-five dollars. We hauled them home, sanded and painted and refinished and restored and repurposed, and we remember. We still use them today.

Then we would make bread. Determined to raise our children on the highly nutritional wheat harvested from where we grew up, we grind the hard red and white spring wheat and shape our own loaves. We make cinnamon rolls. Sometimes we roll the dough into various sizes of balls and form them into teddy bears. We use raisins for eyes. We pat dough into crust for the pizza we will make for dinner. We stir up our favorite Super-Friday-Family-Fun-Night Chocolate Cake and choose a movie to watch or a game to play.

Then, "Dad, read me a story that is not in a book!"

"Tell us again, Dad!" "Pleeeeease, Dad!" "Just one more, Dad!"

When we moved out of this house and I had cleaned every inch, I placed a large bouquet of red tulips in the kitchen for the new owners and lots of blow bubbles for the children moving in. I sat in the middle of the most beautiful, more than one-hundred-year-old hardwood maple floors I had ever seen and remembered.

Remembered how you and I had pulled up the carpet and a million staples and painstakingly refinished every inch. How we had to stay off of them while the stain and the polyurethane dried, coat after coat after coat.

Finally—the last coat set to dry downstairs, we took the kids upstairs and all piled onto the bed in the guest bedroom—known as the Sheep Room. As they fell asleep, sprawled out all over us, we watched the movie *Dr. Zhivago*. On Thanksgiving. That was one of the most thankful times of my whole life.

I sat in the middle of the most beautiful maple hardwood floors I had ever seen and remembered. So many stories. So much joy. Those years had made a mark on this woman's life that is not easily removed. She has never forgotten, saving it all deep and safe inside herself.

Your enthusiasm for building began to wiggle its way into me. You worked at transposing the visions in your head into drawing plans with pencil on paper. I delighted in watching you think and sketch and work at the antique drafting table Michael had worked hard to refinish.

I came to realize what I wanted most was you.

Our stories are embedded in us much more than the walls of any one place.

It had been five years since Michael had died. I consult the calendar and the clock as required regarding obligations and schedules, otherwise my concept of time is entirely nebulous. Vague. Fuzzy. Formless. How to measure five years? It seems like yesterday that he died. It seems like forever since we have touched him or talked with him. His friends were beginning to graduate from college and get married.

Have I ever told you that Michael told me he intended to ask you to be his best man?

When we talk about the home where you grew up and I wonder what it was like for you not to have known your dad, you tell me it is difficult to know what you have not known. Our kids' stories have been written so differently. They have known and been known by you. They have loved and been loved by you. What are the stories they will tell when asked about you? They have a poignant collection to choose from.

As Michael's death has marked Tyler and Megan's lives in ways I struggle yet to comprehend, I have watched you be with them and be for them—loving them with a firmly embedded affection that has anchored and supported them their entire lives. You have deeply impacted them, and they have deeply impacted you, for life. They are about to leave home and I wonder … how they will be.

There is a ravine I pass by and remember the day Tyler passed by this same ravine and stopped to help a police officer break out a window in order to get to the driver, who had veered off the road while having a heart attack. All medical efforts failed. The man was pronounced dead. Right there. In a ravine. In the middle of town.

The pronouncement of death is a solemnly noticeable event. Watching death provoked something vital in Tyler that day. In a ravine, in the middle of town. He spoke eloquently about knowing what it feels like when the brother you love dies in a car crash and how much he wanted to help, and how much he wished that man would live. Hidden words he had been holding for so long somewhere deep inside came seeping out from his permeable heart. Saturated in awful-beautiful.

You listen to his hidden words, and you have always loved him in awful and in beautiful.

The house quiets without bikes and soccer balls and drums and friends always hungry for nachos and "love ya, mom" notes left on the kitchen counter.

The house quiets without him.

I play music loud.

Upon returning from a season working in Antarctica, Megan decided to finish college in New Zealand. I will never forget the wild day we took her to the airport. Our youngest. The last to leave the nest. This whole empty-nest thing was not working out like I had planned. I knew as I watched her board that plane for the other side of the world that my world had changed forever. She would never be coming home in the same way again.

The words she left on my pillow are not last words, but they would be the perfect ones. They are lasting words. Enduring words. Sacred words. I read them again and again through hot, blurring tears. She begins with the Mary Oliver quote from our dining room wall: *"Tell me, what is it you plan to do with your one wild and precious life?"* What does a daughter say to her mother who has...

I crawled up on her bed, so excited for her life, cried inconsolably and missed her like crazy. I felt so empty but so full all at the same time. Our thirteen-year-old dog, a Westie named Lindsay, had died just a few days before. The three of us spent the last night of her life together in this bed, Megan and I comforting Lindsay and letting her know we loved her. She was a faithful friend her whole life to our whole family, and we will miss her. We, in our shared stories of love and loss, have become woven one right into the other.

She must leave.

Brave and courageous.

The space where she will not be tonight will be raging quiet without her. There will be no curling up together with our dog and giving each other back rubs. She will still be on that plane—8,263.2 miles or 13,298.4 kilometers or 7,175.8 nautical miles. However you measure it, more than an eighteen-hour flight away. Crossing the equator, that great circle of the earth dividing the northern and southern hemispheres.

Dividing us.

I must stay.

Brave and courageous.

She left lasting love words on your pillow too. "As I take a new turn in my life, I can't leave without writing some thoughts for a father who has been a true inspiration for his daughter…"

Pillows can hold a lot of words and a lot of tears and a whole head heavy-full of thoughts all at the same time.

"There is no safe investment. To love at all is to be vulnerable. Love anything, and your heart will certainly be wrung, and possibly broken. If you want to make sure of keeping it intact, you must give your heart to no one, not even an animal." —C. S. Lewis.

Love anything and your heart will certainly be wrung. Squeezed and twisted and spun.

In life and in death and in love my heart is spinning, and I guess I am still not thickened up enough.

Unsafe investments. That's what we are.

Here we are—back to you and me.

Mr. and Mrs.

We have and we hold.

The dynamics of our family are drastically rearranged with one of us dead and the rest of us living in different places. It is taking an unmeasurable amount of time for the four of us to navigate the peculiar changes.

We hold on tight and wonder how to let go all at the same time.

"You will make new memories," was a comment we heard often. I do not ever want to forget the old ones. Memory is a strange and unreliable thing.

We won't forget, will we? We must never forget.

We are much more alive than categorized and compartmental-ized stories of old and new. Before and after. Then and now. We occupy all of our story in all of our being—an ongoing story in the context of a larger ongoing story. The beautiful and the awful. They are intermingled from the whole of our lives. We struggle with holding them both but refuse to dismiss either.

We will live more of both. We will live more joy. More sorrow. More comedy. More tragedy. More life. More death. More love. There is so much mystery to life that I do not understand. Things are not as they seem. *"I would not give a fig for the simplicity on this side of complexity, but I would give my life for the simplicity on the other side of complexity." —Oliver Wendell Holmes.*

You and I will move out of the charming Cape Cod on the quaint, tree-lined street that solidly held all of us like a cradle for thirteen growing-up years, taking the beautiful things, our memories and stories, right along with us.

I think I can find a sample of that golf room wallpaper somewhere.

Building

TWO

☙

"Architecture is the thoughtful making of a space."
—Louis Kahn

W E WENT TO SEE THE GROUND where we would build. You told me the streets in the neighborhood would have the names of famous gardens around the world. Our street would be called Straffan, which means stream, a garden located in Kildare, Ireland. The houses would have the names of trees. You named ours Linden Haus after the enormous linden tree in the backyard of the charming Cape Cod around which our family had formed years of lively memories.

We have raked up thousands of linden leaves. Linden leaves are glossy and smooth. They are lustrously dark green and distinctly shaped like a heart. It is your heart that I see, embracing the way we live and breathe together, emulated in architecture.

Listening to music by Brulè, one of my favorite music groups, I am thinking about how a composer chooses each note for each instrument and arranges them into a melodious, integrated whole.

An entire language is dedicated to musically communicate the intended experience the composer desires for the listener.

Architecture also has an entire language all its own.

The dwelling, the living of people, is what dictates the form of design. Harmony and rhythm are essential, underlying notions of any type of art, including architecture. The art of architecture is intimately connected with people's daily lives—as they live in it—all of their lives, from the day they are born until the day they die.

Remember when the children were young and formed dwellings of their own? They built rooms with sheets and blankets and wooden clothes pins—like a big tent. Sometimes they used cardboard boxes out in the yard and lots of duct tape. They gathered up flashlights, pillows, more blankets, water, peanut butter sandwiches, and popcorn. They created art and hung it on the walls. They made up addresses and designed envelopes and postage stamps. They wrote and delivered letters. Stuffed animals, music, books, and games contributed to the order and harmony of their homey surroundings.

Perceptively attuned to harmony, rhythm, proportion, scale, materials, textures, light-that-is-constantly-changing, colors, and primarily people, you have created a composition in the form of a home that is an integrated whole—bringing order and relation of many parts into the surroundings intimately connected with our lives.

What you have communicated to me is so beautiful.

You have drawn me in—shaping parts of me as you shape a home for us.

You have architecturally arranged a melodious, integrated whole.

I hear you.

Your vision for the people who dwell inside has penetrated my heart deeply.

An integrated whole, it is a symphony of spaces. It is a poem. A sculpture. A work of art.

Some art is not easily explained. Sometimes it must be experienced personally. *"Build your life as you would build a work of art."* —*Rabbi Abraham Joshua Heschel.* What is the life we are building?

We are no strangers to being sad, you and me. Our lives have been so out of order the past several years, all parted out, seemingly separated from any sense of an integrated whole. Clashing colors, giving no relief in any form. Visually unbalanced, like we might fall off the precarious line we walk at any point along the way. Harsh, quavering light. Unprotected voids. Uncomfortable temperatures. No point for our blurry eyes to rest. As the house was being constructed, I thought a lot about how our deconstructed selves were in process of being reconstructed. A pounding, messy journey.

We were coming to discover there was something solid being built in us. Something solidly real that would not be easily destroyed, no matter how much more was to come.

The reconstruction of our selves brought with it opportunity for restoration of what had been damaged in our relationship. Our love is no longer simple or naive. It is love that has battled with death. In spite of the fact that we remain tainted with self-centeredness, we have vigorously accompanied each other in dying to "self" in many ways.

Unexpected, isn't it, while at our very worst, in the middle of intense grief and sorrow, depression, and heartache, something within each of us came to want to love the other at astonishingly deeper levels than ever before. No matter the cost to our selves.

You have awakened me to see, hear, and feel things I have never seen, heard, or felt before. To have and to hold. In sickness and in health. For richer or for poorer. To love and to cherish. Two become one, naked and unashamed. In life. In death. In love.

Full nest.

Or empty nest.

Death has not parted us yet.

You began to move away from crossword puzzles and toward me, embracing and enfolding my hibernating heart. Even as I had spun a prickly protective covering about myself in a cocoon of mourning, you surrounded me with you and waited. For me to unseal myself.

A quote from Thomas Merton on one of our walls reads: *"Art allows us to both find ourselves and lose ourselves at the same time."* These words take on fresh meaning as we live them out together.

Losing.

Finding.

Living.

Dying.

Building.

Relationship.

A life.

A work of art.

Watching you work, I observe you plan functional space, but as you plan space, you imagine and intend so much more. You think particularly hard about how the people who live in the space will place significant meaning in the life experiences that unfold there.

You concern yourself not just with physical things in and of themselves but how people interact with their physical surroundings and with each other. Little girls looking out at the stars from their bedroom windows. Families roasting marshmallows in the backyard. Making teddy bear bread and pizzas together in the kitchen. Dads reading stories that aren't in books in family rooms. You contemplate subtle enhancements that inject beauty and richness into architectural design, into life.

I ask a lot of questions. With a gentle glimmer in your eye and a pencil in your hand, you always bring me back to the essential idea of the building and how we can reinforce the expression of that. You teach me about shapes and forms you refer to as gestalt: our comprehension of visual shapes, or of melodies in music, comes as a total and integrated response. Typically, we tend not to deduce individual properties from the sum of its parts. But you do. As you design, you pay serious attention to every single part because it will affect how people live in the space as a whole. The whole is greater than the sum of its parts.

You tell me that it is the dialogue of the materials that we choose, not the materials themselves, that will create the conversation we want to live in. Beauty flows from harmonious relationships—more than from just the components themselves.

Relationships and dialogue and conversation are massively significant and touching things…

"Build your life as you would build a work of art."

You built me architectural models out of foam core and mat board. You built furniture to scale that looked just like ours—including the mission-style sofa I dragged home from the thrift store. We played with different arrangements, like in a dollhouse. You even made little tiny trees in little tiny clay pots for the terrace.

When I had questions, you pulled out your ready roll of bum-wad vellum paper and pencil and drew me a picture. Literally.

I delighted in your sketching and drawing and the engaging way you looked me in the eye while expressing your visionary thoughts behind why you designed the way you did.

While you focus on solid construction, you never lose sight of your vision for the final goal of the space you intend to sculpt or how people might interface with and interact in it. You never lose sight of the essential idea of the building and how we can reinforce the expression of that.

I am falling in love with you all over again.

It has not so much to do with the house.

It is the life that we are building.

How will we reinforce the expression of that?

Nonverbal language communicates at least as explicitly as verbal communication.

The language of building structures, patterns of order and of people, are read and interpreted by each of us every day. We integrate data from all of our senses and intuitions and perceptions and comprehensions to form an overall essence of our surroundings.

How space is defined is an essential, communicative part of architectural language. Along with solid spaces there are fluid spaces forming voids—empty space within the solid space—like the space between words in a sentence. What is not there is as important as what is there. Together they contribute to an artistic arrangement of parts that make the composition of the whole not only more easy to comprehend but more beautiful as well. Solid and void work together to set the mood of a place, drawing us to the way it looks and also inspiring in us a certain way of life.

A life of relationships and dialogue and conversation.

What would approachable or inviting look like emanated in a human being? Do we say things before we actually say things?

Can a person be like a place in some ways? If we were to describe each other using metaphorical images of building materials, colors, light, and shadow, what would our descriptions be like?

Building
THREE
‿

"Imagine yourself as a living house. God comes in to rebuild that house. At first, perhaps, you can understand what He is doing. He is getting the drains right and stopping the leaks in the roof and so on; you knew that those jobs needed doing and so you are not surprised. But presently He starts knocking the house about in a way that hurts abominably and does not seem to make sense. What on earth is He up to? The explanation is that He is building quite a different house from the one you thought of—throwing out a new wing here, putting on an extra floor there, running up towers, making courtyards. You thought you were being made into a decent little cottage: but He is building a palace. He intends to come and live in it Himself."

—C. S. Lewis, *Mere Christianity*

O FTEN PERCEIVED AS A STALWART SYMBOL of shelter, the roof is the least accessible part of a building and often goes mostly unnoticed. That is, until it becomes damaged, leaks, or caves in. The most important parts of a roof are the supporting structure, typically long beams of a material that will be strong under tension, and the outer skin, which can be various materials. It varies around the world, but where we live asphalt shingles are typical, as is a pitched or gable shape. Roofs need to repel a lot of water, which must be directed in a suitable way or it will cause moisture and ventilation problems. Without a roof, we are left out in the wide open, vulnerably exposed, unsheltered and unprotected from harsh elements.

A roof, together with its structural elements, encloses, encompasses, enwraps a building. In your visionary, relational mind the roof is an integral part of the building—containing, embracing, and encircling those it shelters. I remember how you grappled with the rooflines. I remember the day you came to your envisioned conclusion and enthusiastically drew it on paper. Nested gables, you called it. The alignment of the gables has a significant impact on the interior two-story floor plan, therefore, a significant impact on the people living inside. A visually balanced, sculpted composition of nested gables on the outside correlates and connects with the sculpting of spaces on the inside. On the people living on the inside.

You offer sheltering to others of your own self.

Without drawing attention to your own difficulties, you have carried a heavy load. You have carried me. Us. You have been a caressing structure of strength in spite of strained tension. Through battering winds and unrelenting storms, you have enfolded me. Encompassing. Embracing. Enwrapping. Your heart presence all around me and with me.

Sometimes as we fall asleep, all tucked in under nested gables, you ask me, "Are you warm? Safe and dry?" Words from a song you liked while in college called *Same Old Lang Syne* by Dan Fogelberg. It is a story partly about a woman who married an Architect. He kept her warm, safe, and dry, but he did not really love her, nor did she love him. I look you in the eye and I know what you are really asking me. You reinforce the expression of the life we are building.

Increasingly cognizant of the enveloping impact of a roof, I hope to be like a roof too.

And a floor.

I walk across it. I mop it every Thursday. I admire its variegated colors of both light and dark. These long, thin, flat pieces of timber with their knots and swirls and imperfections reveal a flowing, life-like graciousness and unpretentiousness. The hickory tree is prized for its hardwood as well as its flavor in smoked meats.

Because of the taproot that goes very deep down into the earth, the hickory tree is extremely wind resistant. It is highly tolerant of summer drought. Its resilient properties make it especially suitable for flooring and furniture and ladder rungs and tool handles —even early golf clubs—products that are subject to stress. The wood of the hickory tree is known for its strength.

I have intimately known your strength. You have graciously and unpretentiously used it to guard and grow relationships, to create ordered beauty out of what could otherwise be only chaos.

Your anchoring roots go deep. Even during the years of drought, you did not let your agonizing disappointment turn into bitterness. Through it all, all these years, you have remained nurturing, developing, and strengthening.

Remember how the dust clouded and swirled around you as you uncomplainingly worked at sanding crusty, uncooperative varnish from the one-hundred-year-old maple wood floors in the Sheep House? In the swirl of dust, in the swirl of life, in the swirl of things that just don't matter, you are a grounding sense of soul strength. *"Things that matter most must never be at the mercy of those that matter least." — Johann Wolfgang Goethe.* When I get all caught up in commotion and confusion, you remind me—sort out what is just swirl from what really matters one hundred years from now, and into eternity.

There is something very deep inside of you that has flowed into the deepest parts of me, and our children. You have revealed the character of God to us in ways that only you, as my husband and their father, can. You have actively loved us in ways that only you can, from the center of your soul.

We build our life.

We build a house.

Brick stands solidly at the entrance. Bonding is the laying of bricks in courses to build a wall by overlapping them for strength. Mortar is the literal bond adhesive enabling the bricks to stick together, ensuring the strength of the structure. There are small openings in the mortar joints called weep holes, designed to allow water to "weep" out from behind the walls. This too contributes to the strength of the structure. Without a way for water to exit, the integrity of the wall would be compromised. The brick is called, in the language of brick, "tumbled," meaning it possesses a kind of weathered look—each one has a unique mark and has been fired in warm clay shades of color, displaying distinct tactile qualities—kind of like us. I like how each one is different, but they all fit together to be so beautiful.

Even when they weep.

An unusually tall wooden door ushers us into what feels like an inner sanctuary.

A refuge.

A comforting place to recharge.

A place to rest from the rest of the world.

Can a person be like a place?

I am completely mesmerized by the way the light dances around in the space. I notice it streaming in at interesting angles. It casts fascinating shadows, forming organic artwork on the warm, earthy color of the walls.

You told me one time that a large part of what drew you to study architecture is the complex interaction between light, shade, and shadow. Captivated by the extraordinary sunset of the evening, we reveled in the crimson-orange-gold light warming and softening every space it touched. Everything glowing beautiful—like it was all on fire but not burning up. "Listen especially close," you whispered, "at dawn and at dusk."

Dawn is unfolding arrival. A beginning. The first sign of something. Birth. Awakening. An opening.

An ending, dusk is shade and shadow. Sun setting. Moon rising. Night falling.

Soul-stirring acoustics from beginning to end.

"Let there be light."

"It is finished."

We walked in glowing beautiful, and you talked to me of light, that we are drawn to light because light is life.

Light is constantly moving during the day. The quantity of light is not as important as the quality because of how the light falls. Light coming into a space from two different directions is most comfortable for conversations because there is less glare around people's faces. Expressions, eye movements, postures, motions of body language, therefore meanings, may be missed under an intensely harsh glare of light.

Light bounces off the glass of windows, stone countertops, wooden floors, and the ceiling. Outside perspectives are enjoyed from inside reflections—like having subtle, natural mirrors—alive with nature in every direction. You can see sky, birds, grass, flowers, trees in all of their glorious, waving motion, clouds changing shapes and formation, all around you—right beside you. How light makes its way into a space at different times of day and throughout the seasons creates entirely different experiences.

In keeping a tight color palette, colors will select themselves based on what the light does. An inspiring means of expression, the light divides and articulates space with inexplicable connections between colors and materials. Materials like wood and stone have natural colors unto themselves, which is an opportunity to let the light intensify their natural beauty, determining the full quality of the space. *"Let's not detract from the natural beauty of the materials and their interplay with the light but instead, exercise restraint." —Jim Berg.*

Long, soft shadows of gray-yellow morning light stream in from an east wall of windows and doors leading out to the terrace, which allows light to reach deep into all areas of the house. You would never know this secret garden exists from the outside. Looking out onto the terrace, you can take pleasure in not only the terrace but at the same time a reflection of the very front windows and outside to the trees in the park across the street.

In 1902 Irving Colburn patented a sheet-glass machine making it possible to mass-produce glass windows. Windows on a house are like eyes on a person. Windows are dynamic in the sense that they provide a relationship with the outside yet at the same time provide a comforting awareness of being enclosed. Windows inspire contemplative perspectives; thoughts about true understanding of the relative importance of things. Fresh ways of looking at the world. Observing. Being aware. Seeing. Discerning. Discovering. Reflecting.

Purposely placed windows have six separate panes on the top, held protectively by wood mullioned frames, and one large pane on the bottom. Smaller panes put us more intimately in touch with the outside. Each pane is like a photo frame intensifying a particular scene outside. There is a scene from one pane. There is a scene from two panes, or three, or four, or all six. Each stands beautifully alone or in any combination with another.

Nature is always in motion—a sense of aliveness in all perspectives. It is like an entire art gallery experience looking out paned windows. Particularly beautiful is the light filtering itself through rustling leaves on the trees and climbing woodbine. Leaves and light and shadow and color and texture dance in organic, untamed joy.

I am so drawn—to You. You are Light. You are the ultimate source of Life. You, God-light, stream into the world, but we wander in darkness. Light brings to light. Light exposes. Uncovers. Unveils. Lays open. Unmasks. Reveals.

Blind and in the dark, we do not see very well. I do not want to live blind and hard and alone and lost in the dark. I want Light to be with and within me. I want You.

You are Light to live by; even the darkness cannot put You out. You came into the world so we could know You and love You and not be dead in the dark, lost in ourselves. You call us out of our caskets and into Light. Why did You? Why do You?

You came into the world to carry a heavy load. To carry a cross. To carry us. To embrace and encircle us. Your heart presence all around us and with us and in us. You are the ultimate source, the taproot, of Life. You create ordered beauty out of what could otherwise be only chaos. I see reflections of You everywhere. You have uniquely formed and fired and shaped and marked each one of us. You have wept over each one of us. You are our sanctuary, our refuge.

You are the beginning and the ending. You are ... the Light and the Life of the world.

Building
FOUR
⌒

"Life is not an illogicality, yet it is a trap for logicians. It looks just a little more mathematical and regular than it is; its exactitude is obvious; but its inexactitude is hidden; its wildness lies in wait."
—G. K. Chesterton

ENTERING THE HOUSE, THE SPACE SEEMS relatively open—but not entirely open. While being in one space, the next layer whispers invitingly—divulging a little bit of itself yet not fully revealing itself. You have built a house of layered spaces. From the very front window you can see through the layers to the very back window. Not directly straight through but little unveilings, glimpses. The light is always moving, offering invitations of its own.

Being the most social, least private space, the dining room is intentionally at the front of the house with windows open toward the street. The low sills provide for a wide view, encompassing both the ground and the horizon, as well as soaring potential for imagining. The layer of soft, simple silk curtains complements the hard of the glass and wood and stone, while offering privacy when wanted.

"Tell me, what is it you plan to do with your one wild and precious life?" —*Mary Oliver.* Words written on the wall stimulate the imagination, curiosity, and conversation of those gathered around the table.

"To feast together is to bear witness to the joy one has at being with his friends. The mere act of eating together, quite apart from a banquet or some other festival occasion, is by its very nature a sign of

friendship and of 'communion.' —*Thomas Merton.* We light candles. Who is not mesmerized by the flirtatious dance of the candle's flame? We play music. *"Music expresses that which cannot be put into words and that which cannot remain silent."* —*Victor Hugo.* We tell stories. We feast on simple food as we feast on each other, bearing witness to great joy.

Being a long, skinny house, ninety-four feet long and twenty feet wide, the layering of spaces breaks up the linear geometry. In the absence of layering, it would be an entirely different space. It would feel long and skinny and be awkwardly broken up by walls and doors in an attempt to create separate rooms. Layers add a distinguishable sense of depth and richness to the entire space.

Moving into the kitchen, the eye stops at the surrounding soffit, breaking up the long and linear. Clearly delineated from the other layers, it is also clearly connected. A relaxed mood is set by relaxed materials. Wood, slate, and copper—markers of enduring patience, solid simplicity, practicality, and artistic playfulness stir up all sorts of excitement in me for chopping, slicing, steaming, sautéing. Grinding. Kneading. Mixing. Blending. Baking. Broiling. Brewing. Pouring. Serving. Chatting. It is a space of endless opportunity for creativity.

Bracing the counter is an antique newel post salvaged from the staircase of a house built in the 1800s. It is similar to the one that was in the Sheep House. And the one in the charming Cape Cod. It stands there, all composed and untroubled, bearing its heavy burden much more elegantly than I have born mine.

Still refinishing and repurposing old things, we are glad to give this fascinating piece of history a new home. I wonder how many hands, young and old, have touched this solid, warm wooden post, hung on tight, trusting it to steady them from falling on the stairs. Whose fingers have gripped it in order to keep their balance as they paused to tell a story or adjust the load of laundry balancing on their hip? Maybe it has served as a firmly fixed footing to huddle up against for a wrenching cry as a strong storm raged within a hallowed life.

A sense of spatial generosity pulsates while moving into the next layer, the sitting room, where the eye is drawn past it and into another layer, the outside terrace. Meaningful conversations and kind gestures between one another have been vital to your vision from the beginning. Popping corn and telling stories by a warm fire. Watching the stars from the terrace.

Built by a carpenter more than one hundred years ago, the fireplace mantelpiece has aged slowly and nobly. It holds its own historical background confidential as well as a myriad of other stories that have been told around enchanting flames. There is an absence of tension in the juxtaposition of old and new. Stories crisscross each other, woven and spun from the past and the present, with emerging life themes common to all.

Above the mantle a Latin proverb reads: DUM SPIRO SPERO. *"As I breathe, I hope."*

As I breathe, I hope.

I hope. I hope. I hope.

On the wall nearby is a quote. *"The way to love anything is to realize that it might be lost." —G. K. Chesterton.* We could sit by the fire chatting about hope and love and losing and finding for hours. We could sit by the fire and not say a word.

Just breathe.

Without intruding, other layers playfully unveil bits of themselves. There is a sense of being connected with other layers and the people in them. It is the layers that create inviting transitions—rather than doors.

Freedom of movement is an important element in how a space "lives and breathes," impacting those who live and breathe in it. The intentional circulation between spaces provides opportunity for nuances of meaning regarding how we want to play or not play, move or not move, talk or not talk. We might want to be all alone. Alone with one other person. Be near others but not intensely involved with them or be an active part of a group. There are a medley of places to sit at various degrees of intimacy and intensity. Friendly degrees of circulation, separation, and togetherness create a house that moves in order that those who live in it can move within a rhythm of spatial, thriving, relational generosity.

There is a sitting space overlooking the fireplace that you call the bridge. Built in the form of a bridge, it is a connecting space from one layer to another. It is a semiprivate place, partially open to other spaces, thereby enabling people to enjoy the fire, smell dinner cooking, hear the music being played, the chatter and laughter of others floating up, yet have a quiet conversation while still being a passive part of the larger gathering.

Metrically poetic—you reinforce the expression of the life we are building—making room for rest, for movement, for play. For conversation. Quiet. Community. Solitude. Listening. Inviting. Engaging.

Parts we need to be whole.

Along with the horizontal layering there is an intersection of vertical layering. The central vertical axis is the staircase. This staircase, in particular, is the organizing element of the house. A staircase is a complex combination of treads, risers, and banisters. It is much more than just a way to get from one floor to another. It is not a dead space of disconnection but a vital part of connection with the other layers. An unusual pattern of textural beauty is woven in combining unexpected materials together, such as the economical strand board walls with sturdy micro lam treads. It is significant that the stairs are without risers. Every stair is open, allowing the eye not to stop but instead to see beyond each individual stair, to embrace other layers of distinct space and, most importantly, to engage with the angle of the light. Always the light is moving, effectively varying subtle nuances in and of the space. Light alone can be the most meaningful element—how the light falls is often the most integral part of a space as other elements are oriented to and organized around it.

Moving from front to back, the layers begin to become more private.

Rather than a door, there is a small landing between one flight of stairs and another that feels like a rest on a sheet of music. Pausing to look out the window into the terrace while passing by is emotionally restorative. There is time—to breathe deep. To hope. To rest your heart.

The rest leads to what might seem like just a long hallway. The eye is drawn to the wall of art at the end, *The Story Book,* painted in

1877 by French artist, father of five William Adolphe Bouguereau.

It is not, however, just a long hallway but a library—a long, skinny space chock-full of books, old cameras, and typewriters. *"Medicine for the Soul."* —the inscription over the door of the Library at Thebes. Indeed, it is.

The first typewriter was invented around 1867 in the United States, but it is believed that a form of typewriter may have been used in Egypt during the time of the Pharaohs. The history, form, and function of old typewriters are fascinating to me. As with the old cameras, I sincerely appreciate that they are highly effective tools for communication, for telling stories. I imagine each one of these typewriters has quite an amazing story of its own. Just think of all the words they have struck onto paper. All around the world. In many different languages. Typists have pounded out personal stories, newspaper stories, business arrangements, and military documents. It was such an important tool to the Navy during World War II that the Royal Typewriter Company produced a certain style of typewriter just for them, along with guns and bullets, propellers, and spare parts for the engines of airplanes.

Ernest Hemingway had a stand specially constructed to hold his Remington typewriter so he could type out his books while standing up. Remington was founded in 1816 as a gun manufacturer. The company produced the first commercial typewriter in 1873.

Children who have never seen a typewriter before are often enamored and unable to break themselves away from exploring the clicking and dinging and the setting of the paper. In their lives they have only known computers. I show them how the keyboard is still arranged the same way on both. They convey to me how much more difficult it would be to lug a typewriter around than a computer. They wonder out loud, incredulously, what people did without the Internet.

Favorite books collected over a lifetime line the shelves. The books about President McKinley I bought at the estate sale on the day Michael died among them. Underneath *The Story*, on the black iron stand it has set on for more than all of my life, is a 1925 *Webster's New International Dictionary of the English Language* from my grandparents' dining room. It holds and defines words I cannot find in other dictionaries.

Cameras of varied vintage and style are tucked in amongst the books. Cameras that have taken photos of flowers and trees and mountains and dogs and water and landscapes and fruit and pastries and crime scenes and babies' first steps and birthday parties and old men with canes and children playing violins. Cameras capturing images of people from various locations all around the world, at diverse points throughout history, personal as well as world events and circumstances, facial expressions, laughter, and tears.

Lifetimes of stories.

On the wall a quote:

"Read me a story that's not in a book." — *Megan Berg, age three.*

While the width of the space is narrow, the vaulted ceiling is high, creating privacy in an open, intriguing way. On the wall above the round, wooden desk is written *"He who does not weep, does not see."* — *Victor Hugo.* Victor Hugo's firstborn, a son, died before turning one year old.

His oldest daughter, falling out of a boat in long, heavy skirts, died at age nineteen in 1843. Her husband died trying to save her from drowning. Hugo found out about their deaths reading the newspaper. Two other sons, one leaving two small children, died at young ages as well. Another daughter lived her life in an institution for the mentally afflicted. By the time *Les Miserables* was published in 1862 Mr. Hugo had intimately known a lot of misery. For 1,222 pages he unravels tragic and beautiful. The law condemns. Love redeems. What is there, but to love one another...

This intense story of very deep insight sits on the shelf where I can see it, medicine for my soul. A reflective reminder of the crippling epiphany conversation with Michael while all tucked into that giant wing chair covered in the deep green tapestry of golf courses from all around the world. The profundity of the question is more profound than ever. The profundity of the answer is growing more profound to me than ever. I weep. More than ever.

I am tenderly aware of how you have drawn me in—designing this layer of library with me on your mind and in your heart. It is relatively private, yet still obscurely open to the spaces around it.

While it might seem like a dead end from the other end, it is not. It is another layer built in the form of a bridge. A connection. A joining. An artistic passageway. Each individual book adds yet another layer. Walking through to the end of the space where *The Story* hangs and the dictionary sits on its stand, the ceiling height changes from high and vaulted to low and flat, adding subtle but significant meaning to the space. Unnoticeable, to the side is a door to our bedroom.

The deeper into the house, the deeper the intimacy gradient, the deeper the privacy.

From our bedroom a balcony with glass doors opens to the terrace. This secret garden, this inner sanctum, enhances the entire whole—lavishing light and shadow, leaking beauty, fresh air, a sense of proportion, a blending sense of separate yet together, a way of seeing. Depending on the light as it moves throughout the day, and the seasons as well as the colors the light chooses, layers bleed together—intensifying the quality of the space. The strong, natural connections seem to enliven the vibrancy of human connections. There is a tree that grows in this outdoor room, not for landscaping purposes but because it forms an important sense of sheltering place. Friends planted an almond tree in Israel in memory of Michael. They explained to us that trees in general, almond trees in particular, are a symbol of hope and joy amid pain and turmoil.

In the peak of autumn a window box attached to the balcony is laden with red-orange lantana flowers spurting big, blue-colored berries and asparagus fern. Little pumpkins nestle in as if they can hide from the soon-coming frost. Your favorite, the woodbine, is turning the most remarkable vibrant red. The ferns have grown to be massive mounds of willowy green. The well-protected leaves of the dogwood tree are slowly changing color. I never tire of the twinkling lights. They move with the rustling leaves, making them flicker like real flame. Through these doors I can vaguely see backwards through the many layers into the sitting room, all the way through the kitchen and out the very front windows of the house to the trees in the park across the street.

Closing the curtains on the glass doors into the terrace makes our bedroom, the space most deep into the house, entirely private.

For the deepest, most private of conversations. You maintain this is a space for resting, renewing, reviving, and restoring. To be emotionally and spiritually strengthened by being alone or by being together. You protect this purpose through the scale of the space, the light, the color of the paint on the walls and ceiling, even the fabrics of the bedding. This room of rest initiates thoughts in me of what rest really means. All around me, and often within me, there seems to be mostly unrest. What would it mean to be in a restful place internally, a restful place in my soul?

I have not forgotten the raw, awful feeling that we would never be restored. Regenerated. Redeemed. That the dark grip of death would grasp and grab at us in a forever stranglehold. A bearing down of unbearable compression. Confined. Unable to move. Trapped in contorted, jittery places without any point of orientation. It felt like it would never, ever, ever be well with our souls.

I remember a time when I was having an extraordinarily difficult time resting, both internally and externally. While sleep seldom came to me, you somehow kept your drowsy eyes, used to falling asleep fast, open late into the night reading me favorite stories from *All Creatures Great And Small, All Things Wise and Wonderful,* and *The Lord God Made Them All,* written by English veterinarian James Herriot. I especially like the ones about Tristan's shenanigans and Mrs. Pumphrey and her spoiled pet Pekinese Tricki Woo, but I love them all. How I would have enjoyed inviting James and Helen, Tristan, Siegfried, Mrs. Hall, Mrs. Pumphrey, Tricki Woo, and her gardener Hodgkins for dinner. I remember one of the children's favorite James Herriot stories was about Moses, a lost black kitten found among the rushes, who ended up nursing from Bertha, a sow feeding her brand-new litter of twelve piglets. Moses grew up thinking he was one of them.

I have never forgotten your spanning—supporting—holding kindness toward me during that qualmish time. Soothing me to sleep, you put your arms around me as you read story after story out loud. Keeping me warm. Safe. And dry. Sharing your pillow, lasting words, enduring words, sacred words. Your eminently graceful, gentle voice rallied rest.

Sometimes you hummed me "our" song, chosen when we were teenagers. "If"—from the record album *The Best of Bread*: "If a picture paints a thousand words, then why can't I paint you ... the words will never show the you I've come to know ... And when my love for life is running dry ... you come and pour yourself on me..."

A sheltering place, I am drawn to and generously held by you.

Additional layers come in the form of the objects, the living expressions, of us. "Remember the context of the simple beauty of natural materials, and the light," you say. "Remember the original design intent. Try not to force things that don't fit. Don't merely decorate, filling space with empty objects that don't mean anything, but remember and consider the things that we thoughtfully want to keep around us." In the space we call home, we want to be surrounded by things that are instinctively meaningful to us, not merely bought off an interior design shelf. There is some sense of our life, history, inclinations, and our stories apparent in the furniture and on the walls.

Ignoring the latest decor fads, you insist the most beautiful decor is what comes straight from our lives—collections of typewriters and cameras and books. Art and furniture that tell a story. Remembrances and photos. In sepia tone, a picture of our three children standing with their backs to the camera by a lake covers an entire wall in your studio. I prize every exploded pixel, each person in their familiar individual stance as I remember enjoying the ways their young eyes, hands, feet, and hearts took in the world.

Each story is another layer of the house.

Of our life.

In the creative acts of building a home, of building a life, of becoming a solid soul rather than a ghost, I am sensing movement from loose and flimsy toward gradual thickening.

We, you and I, two-have-become-one, have become so integrated we are becoming a gestalt of our own. Our whole is greater than the sum of our parts. Our structures, layer by relational layer, are being thickened up, made stronger against disturbing forces.

I read somewhere that much of Bach's music was composed to be played in St. Thomas church in Leipzig. There was a lot of wood in

that church. The wood absorbed sound, greatly reducing the reverberation that helped create the acoustics that made possible much more
intricate music than could have been enjoyed otherwise.

You are like the wood in that church to me.

As an Architect, a pattern thinker, creating ordered beauty out
of what could otherwise be chaos, the ways in which you never lose
sight of the essential idea of the building and how you can reinforce
the expression of that is congruent with the ways in which you never
lose sight of the life we are building and how we can reinforce the
expression of that.

Layers add a distinguishable sense of depth and
richness to a life.

You are a deeply layered man who has added unfathomable
richness to my life: Generosity. Harmony. Playfulness. Courtesy. Kind-
ness. Faithful. Friend. Strengthening. Beauty. Wisdom. Forthrightness.
Quiet. Open. Builder of bridges. Considerate. Welcoming. Light.
Healer. Solemn. Grace. Authentic. Joy. Willing to wait. Wit. Sorrow.
Remembering. Forgetting. Father. Compassionate. Mindful of what
matters. Forbearance. Hospitality. Color. Courage. Texture. Artist.
Grief. Genuine. Tears. Patient with people. Hope. Gracious. Humble.
Husband. Laughter. Tenderhearted. God's strong hand is on you. Calm.
Gratitude. Sacrifice. Struggle. Creative. Curious. Life is holy with mean-
ing. Layer upon layer.

I remember well that moment I met you at the newspaper
rack. In the library. Your face holds much more story now. *"Are we not
like two volumes of one book?"* —*Marceline Desbordes-Valmore.* Your
shoulders are broader. Your hair has come from chocolaty brown to
silvery gray. You have the same smiling, expressive blue eyes. You are
still quiet and tender, but now girded by an intense substructure of
depth underneath.

Your heart is more alive now than ever.

I am more in love with you now than ever.

Pliable and porous serve as the best acoustic insulators—the
most absorbing—as opposed to dense and impenetrable.

Pliable and porous, the ways you have absorbed ... drawn

me and our children in, engaged with us, enwrapped us ... reducing the reverberation ... the noise, the rumble, the swirl of things that just don't matter ... making possible a more beautiful taking-in, spilling-out, messy-wonderful life.

Layer upon relational layer.

Unraveling joys and sorrows.

What is there ... but to love one another?

The way to love anything is to realize it might be lost.

"I can't believe I get you."

Love as Strong as Death

ONE

"Love is not blind. That is the last thing that it is.
Love is bound and the more it is bound the less it is blind."

—G. K. Chesterton

I HAVE DONE A LOT OF WEEPING and am beginning to be able to see. The blurring can be like a blinding. The dark. Unblinded me.

God is always there.

Here.

Even in the dark.

In all of His boundlessness.

He chooses to be bound to me. To you. Encircling, strengthening us at the core of our souls, He expresses His love, boundlessly.

Love. That is stronger than death.

Changes the meaning of death.

How is it that I could be stiff or selfish—stingy with this kind of love?

I am.

Forever bound in Him, can I be boundless in my expression of love too?

Unblinded dying for another is what must be done in really and truly, not seemingly, loving people.

People can be difficult to love.

I am difficult to love.

He sees me.

And loves me.

I want to see Him.

And love too.

"This is My Son, marked by My love, focus of all My delight."

—2 Peter 1:17, The Message.

Marked by My love. That is stronger than death.

Focus of all my delight.

Forever.

Bound.

He wasn't obligated to be bound to us. He wanted to be. Like you, and me. We were not obligated to be bound to each other. We wanted to be. "Will you marry me?" You chose me, and I chose you. We were not looking to be free from each other; more than anything we wanted to be bound, secured, never-let-go-fastened-together until death parts us. We looked each other in the eye and made a vow. A solemn promise.

All tethered and tangled together, we were blind for a while. Bound and (self) determined, the honeymoon came to an eye-opening end. Two-became-one while still being two.

Unlike us, the Son of Man has never been blind. He is love, fully, completely, entirely bound. Secure. Never-lets-go-fastened-together. Fully determined to give His life in order for us to have life. Death will not part us but be the way for us to be together eternally. Always inviting, He requests we follow Him.

In unblinded dying.

Love that is bound is not stingy but gives itself away.

In the losing is the finding.

We, you and me, have lost, and we have found.

"Die before you die. There is no chance after." —C. S. Lewis. We are still discovering all the ways one must die to self-love, unblindingly loving others. There is a lot more self in a self than we realized. What seemingly crumpled and crushed our lives, crumpled and crushed us in the worst way we could imagine, is in some ways also our greatest gift. The Invitation of the Most Precious Kind has everything to do with living more from our redeemed, relational souls than from our selves. While living inside all the crumpled and crushed, it seemed there was nothing that could be stronger than death. In the dark is where I saw the dark in me. It had been a blind spot. The *un*. A lack of vision. The death and new life that has come to our souls will one day come to our bodies. A broader perspective regarding tragedy and evil has made us more somber people; we see life differently now. On the brink of death, life did not just go on; it has become much deeper, and we have become deeper souled, living with and in the light and the dark, the joy and the sorrow. We laugh more, and we cry more. Sometimes at the same time, not in a neutralizing sense but in each a more fervent sense.

I wonder—would there be love if there were no death?

Mostly skin and bones yet her heart huge, I remember how our friend, whom I regarded with deep affection, valiantly fought death. Even her gums were shrinking. This made her dentures painful to wear, especially when trying to eat, even if she felt hungry, which she hardly ever did. While at a chemotherapy treatment one afternoon in a conversation with the doctor regarding food, he asked her if she liked wine. She said she did. We stopped to get some on the way home. I asked her if she liked red or white. White, she said. "Will you join me for lunch? White wine is the menu," she chuckled through her hand-held synthesizer where her voice box used to be, still a twinkle in her eye. Served in dainty, fragile glasses from her extensive, very fine antique collection, we warm-heartedly toasted our friendship. It became apparent that she would not be able to drink her lunch any more than she could eat it.

Instead, we sat at the kitchen table and watched two mice eat the cat food. She would not let me get rid of the mice. She wanted them to live.

She wanted to live.

We arrived at the hospital later that week for an overnight treatment. Settled in bed, hooked up to all sorts of tubes channeling liquid medicine, she shivered cold. I got a heated blanket from the nurse and tucked it in all around. Still, she shivered cold, so I got another heated blanket. Still, she shivered cold. Somehow we had forgotten to pack her warm socks. I was wearing warm socks with my boots, so I asked her if she wanted mine. She did.

Still, she shivered cold.

I climbed into bed with her, and the tubes, and the heated blankets. I gently snuggled up to her and wrapped my arms around her; my beautiful-friend-gift. She stopped shivering. Amongst the web of dripping tubes we lay there and talked about what it is like to die. Aware death was imminent, she told me she felt very afraid. Very afraid. On the shared hospital-white pillow, intermingled tears interlaced with almost-last words. Enduring words. Sacred words.

"I love you."

Internally struggling, she was deciding if she believed in God or not. If the Gospel is true or not. *"You never know how much you really believe anything until its truth or falsehood becomes a matter of life and death to you." —C. S. Lewis.* Lying there with her, it struck me like lightning that when we die, we die alone. We die by ourselves. No one can do it for us. Can we know the ultimate true meaning of life without knowing the ultimate true meaning of death? What would love mean without death? Would it be the same?

"This is My Son, marked by My love, focus of all My delight." —2 Peter 1:17, The Message. You are marked by this same love, my dear, dear friend. God's love is not blind. That is the last thing that it is. He sees our sin. How we insist life be on our terms, how we harm each other in the ways we relate, how we attempt to use Him as a

means to other things, but He does not turn away from us. He turns toward us. He is bound—suffered and sacrificed—substituted His life for our lives so that we could have life forever with Him. To live, as He lived and died, is to die to our self-centered self, to love others with eternal-centered love, like He loves us. This is love that changes the meaning of death. The ultimate true meaning of life. You want to live. You want to love. Will you see how much He loves you? Will you, unblindingly, say yes?

To His bound, unblinded, sacrificial love that is stronger than death.

Love as Strong as Death

TWO

~

"The striking thing about the Precious Blood is the bond it establishes between love and suffering in our experience, a bond that has become so close that we have come to think of suffering accepted by joy as the most authentic sign of love with any depth at all."

—Gabriel Marcel

WE STAND IN THE GARDEN, IN front of the Tomb of Joseph of Arimathea. There has been some dispute over the location of the actual tomb. Is it here? Or at the church of the Holy Sepulcher? It is a small distance apart. We duck our heads low and enter. It is dark and quiet.

We had come to explore Israel with friends. To walk where Jesus walked. After being inside the tomb, we celebrate communion together. We sing. Others are singing too. French. African. Asian. The sun is beginning to set. "Listen especially close," you had whispered to me long ago, "at dawn and at dusk." Soul-stirring acoustics from beginning to end... It is time for us to leave, but I can hardly move. I too have been the mother weeping at the grave of her firstborn, a son.

I listen especially close as the sun begins its descent.

Can you even imagine... Can you hear the passionate embrace days later upon seeing that He is alive? And that He is not only her son but also her Savior?

"This is My body, given for you." "This is My blood, shed for you." "Do this, in remembrance of Me." How is it that we could ever forget?

Just six miles away in the town of Bethlehem we visit the oldest church in Israel, built over the place where Jesus was born. It is named Church of the Nativity, meaning "cave of birth." I hear Joseph affectionately tending to Mary. I hear jubilant birthing cries from mother and child. I hear careful commotion in cutting the umbilical cord. Did they rub their baby with salt, typically used at that time as a disinfectant? Calm, comforting voices and soothing, secure hands wrap the baby in swaddling clothes from belly button to toes, believing that rigorous movement would be harmful to soft bones. I hear them making the manger soft. I hear holding and hugging and tears of great joy falling down faces and tender exchanges of gentleness between husband and wife. I hear hearts beating strong. The palpable awe of miracle, life, hope. The-extraordinary-overwhelming-sacred-interruption-holy-God-given-promise-kairos-time.

Back in Jerusalem, walking through the oldest, largest cemetery in Israel, we entered the Mount of Olives, known as Garden of Gethsemane—meaning "oil press." Located on a very busy road, it was anything but the quiet I had imagined it to be. Cars and trucks were screeching and screaming. Street vendors were selling everything from camera photo chips to olive branches, bags and beads, hats and shirts. Cars were coming and going, practically running head-on into each other or us on the narrow cobblestone streets.

I feel the pressed. The squeezed.

In spite of all the crazy commotion, I was gripped by the sounds. Jesus praying, with a great deal of strength. Sweating. Struggling. Waking sleeping friends three different times. His friends trying to stay awake but not. His insides churning. "Father, Your will be done, not mine." A hollow-hearted kiss and tell. Thirty jingly pieces of silver, the price of a slave. Someone's ear being sliced right off. Blood spurting. A forgiving. A healing. Swords and clubs swinging in raging hands and hearts. Olives falling on the ground. The rustling of leaves. Night coming. A rooster crowing. Again. And again. Lots and lots of crying. Lots and lots of slapping around. Loud internal determination to carry out His holy mission.

"Non novi illum."

The Latin inscription on a statue near the house of Caiaphas, the high priest presiding over the trial of Jesus.

"I do not know Him."

"I was not with Him."

"He is not my friend."

Is that my voice I hear?

Or someone else's?

What dreadful depravity thought up the idea of crucifixion? Inflicting the most torture possible before the person dies a most horrific death. Have I considered myself to be part of such depravity? In the severe unblinding I am coming to see that I am.

The brutal scourging, beating bloody. The crown of thorns. People screaming for a killing. The cross beam laid on His shoulders to be carried to the execution place. The stripping. Jeering soldiers dividing the clothing. A mocking, purple robe. Anguish pressing hard into His soul. "Father, forgive them." Laid out on the ground, nails pounded into His wrists and feet. His mother watching. Listening. Her heart thumping so hard on her inside you could see it on her outside. Her soul bleeding kindred red. A criminal on either side. A sign hung over Him: THIS IS THE KING OF THE JEWS. Exposed. Exhaustion. Led like a lamb to slaughter. Darkness covered the whole land. Oh, the battle raging in His soul. I cannot comprehend the anguish ripping through the Father and the Son. "Father, into your hands I commit my Spirit." Lasting words. Enduring words. Sacred words... Together the Father and the Son prevailing over sin's power, sacrificing, suffering for those they love, so that we could enjoy relationship with them forever.

The pouring of a Life, in a dying.

Who would have thought God's saving power would look like this?
—*Isaiah 53:1, The Message.*

Do we comprehend and understand the full implication of redemption without comprehending and understanding the full impact of the corruption of sin?

A symbol of shame, You make the cross Yours as a symbol of suffering-self-sacrifice and offer it to us as a shared symbol of mystical union

*with You. Dead to self-centeredness. Alive to You, awakened to love
that is eternally centered in the Trinity of Father, Son, and Spirit. You
breathe life into us, make us alive with Your own life.*

The crippling epiphany. Seeing difficult and disturbing things
we have not seen before. The cross reveals the immense gravity of sin—
the defilement of love. Do I really see all the ways I defile love? The cross
reveals the most profound, immense gravity of sacrificial love—love
that is stronger than even death. Love that chooses to love even though
it costs your life. The cross is a heart-rending, soul-stirring, dangerous
place. It is not the place for ghost mothers and their strangling-selfish-
stingy sort of love, insisting on illusional safety, demanding God be the
means to what it is they think they want. That kind of love is destructible, and death will destroy it. Not even death can destroy eternal love;
it is unbreakable. Enduring. Everlasting. Undying. Inextinguishable.
Imperishable. It is indestructible.

*It is You. And You love us like this. And You ache for us to
love You like this. And You yearn for us to love each other like this.*

*Maybe the only way to know You in this place is in this place.
You invite us to follow You. Burgeoning invitation. To love others with
this indestructible kind of love with which You love us. To suffer. To
bleed for someone else. You want us to join You in this holy, sacred
place.*

You want us to join You?
To know You in this holy sacred place?

On a Tuesday morning I, in dire disequilibrium, missing
Michael, Tom asked me what I thought Michael might say to me if he
could. His warm, witty demeanor came to mind; I was not sure about
what he might say. Maybe, Tom said, Michael might say, "Offer to others
what you have offered to me. Love others like you have loved me." My
initial thought was—how could I? "He is my son." God unmistakably
marked me forever with those words. They are seared into my soul.
For that is precisely what He does. *"This is My Son. Do you see My Son?
Love each other as I love Him and He loves Me. He is the focus of all My
delight. Delight yourself in Him."* We are marked by this same love. He

delights in us. Enjoys us. We are so loved. So wanted. He never says, "I don't know what to do with you." He always says, "Will you see how much I love you?" God loves us with the same sacrificial, eternal love that He loves His Son.

That is what God did. That is what God still does. That is what God will always do. I am ever-so-gradually-being-thickened-up, slowly discovering that I *can* love others with the same love God loves me. I like my mask less and less every day. It is exhausting being someone I am really not. Sometimes fear strangles me, and I strangle others. The thing about real love is that it can only come from what is real you. No matter what it costs you. Real love is always a spilling of blood. It is a very great suffering. It is a very great sacred joy.

Eternal, sacrificial, undying love is love that has battled death, and it is bound—in both suffering and joy. The shared symbol of our mystical union with Christ, the most authentic sign of love with any depth at all.

Love as Strong as Death
THREE
✑

"The grace of God means something like: Here is your life. You might never have been, but you are because the party wouldn't have been complete without you. Here is the world. Beautiful and terrible things will happen. Don't be afraid. I am with you. Nothing can ever separate us. It's for you I created the universe. I love you. There's only one catch. Like any other gift, the gift of grace can be yours only if you'll reach out and take it. Maybe being able to reach out and take it is a gift too."

—Frederick Buechner

PHYSICAL DEATH IS IMMINENT TO US ALL. So many people have told us that experiencing the death of a child is the worst of all tragedies. Neither you nor I have ever said that. Human beings made in the image of God all around the world have suffered unimaginable tragedies. People have known unbearable pain and sorrow in a myriad of ways. What kind of measuring system can say one is worse than another? Rather than trying to measure or compare tragedies, can we gather at the cross in our individual pain and sorrow, whatever that is, and as we enter into ours, we enter into His and become more somehow? Absorb more deeply the sorrow, but also the ability to love more deeply in bearing with and being with one another in that place? It would be foolish of us to pick or choose which ones we think we could bear or which ones we think we could never bear. Can we really know the depth of heartache that people go through?

The dreadful heartache of what was a very terrible tragedy to us in our world is what awakened us to a deeper reality in God's world. In amazing grace He connected with us in tender ways we did not expect. How we want to live is intimately joined with how we want to die. We are discovering we are most truly alive, even if in heart-wrenching pain, when, without holding back, we die to self-centered protective ways of thinking and relating, which frees us to love with the kind of love that is eternal.

In the midst of these relentless, core-to-core confrontations regarding life, death, and love, God has poured more life into me than I have ever known, or thought I could ever hold.

Where my heart beats and bleeds for others is where I most want to live—as a real, relational soul, not a false self. Fake has become excessively familiar in our culture. Simulated wood. Imitation jewels. Forged documents. Counterfeit money. Reproduction antiques. Knock-off designer boots and bags. Phony personalities. Real love—undying, eternal love—spills out from a relational soul—an undying, eternal soul. There is no faking that.

Contraries may be more fully known by contraries. *"The only safe place outside of heaven where you can be perfectly safe from all the dangers of love is hell."* —C. S. Lewis.

We live and breathe, laugh and cry in the deepest parts of our being within the context of contraries. We too become more fully known through them. Our real and our fake. The dark and the light. Harmony and discord. Our yes and our no. The sought out. The forsaken. In the quiet. In the disturbed. Strong and weak. Bound and unbound. What is safe? What is dangerous? Which are we? We are both. Calloused and compassionate. Blinded. Seeing. Being seen, or not. For good or for evil. The absence. The presence. The something or the nothing. In empty and in full. Hard and soft. Belief and unbelief. Hope and despair. In awful and in beautiful. The holy. The unholy. With certainty and with uncertainty. Bursting with songs of joy. Bursting with anger. The calm. The chaos. In lost and in found. In ordinary chronos. In extraordinary kairos. In life and in death.

The profundity of the question: the immense gravity of relational sin.

The profundity of the Three-in-One-God who answers: the immense gravity of the relationality of the Cross.

You remember Your intentions for people, and You never lose sight of Your vision for the relational soul You intend to sculpt; and, without ever growing weak or weary, You tirelessly reinforce Your expression of that. You are committed to making us holy as You are holy. Not just nice, improved versions of our old selves but vitally transformed; redeemed into our most true souls. Lovers who have battled death and emerge fully, generously alive—passionate lovers. Like You. You love us like You love Your own Son, and You invite us into that same place, which is very different from the way the culture that surrounds us defines and expresses love. I have held Your teaching inside of me for most of my life. But I could not have fully imagined Your intentions or comprehended Your vision for those You love would look like this. "I can't believe I get You." Feeling the need to lean against a wall, I want to lean into You. How to breathe in so much terrible beautiful?

As I breathe ... I hope...

A futile hope, a hope that might make you feel better even if it wasn't really true, would be no hope at all. The hard things that happen to us may seem like a brutal pass-or-fail test from a puppet-god with a heart of chiseled stone. The hard things that happen to us are not tests as much as they are invitation from God, who has entered into death with us in immense sorrow, grief, anger, and with a heart of love so fervently intense we can hardly comprehend it. Invitation from God, whose blood was shed and whose bright glory has risen for us in eternal love—a language wholly its unfractured own in its purity, intenseness, selflessness, and fidelity. Invitation from God, who desires and seeks soul-to-soul spiritual affection.

Love is patient, love is kind.

It does not envy, it does not boast, it is not proud.

It is not rude, it is not self-seeking, it is not easily angered, it keeps no record of wrongs.

Love does not delight in evil but rejoices with the truth.

It always protects, always trusts, always hopes, always perseveres.

Love never fails.

—*1 Corinthians 13:4-8, New International Version.*

What we might call unwanted interruptions hold stretching potential to become Invitations of the Most Precious Kind.

You invite us to this place so that we can know You in this place. In the joy and in the sorrow of every place we can relate with You. There is no place where we cannot know You and love You, and know others and love others, with love that has battled death. It can be well with our soul, the relational soul that You are sculpting and transforming and loving with the only kind of love that is stronger than death.

This is how we know what love is: Jesus Christ laid down His life for us. And we ought to lay down our lives for our brothers.

—*1 John 3:16, New International Version.*

I thought I would literally die when Michael died. How could I just go on breathing when he wasn't?

The violent blast. A destructive wave of highly compressed air, squeezing and pressing and flattening.

The suffocating dust clouds of fine powder. Carried by the tainted air, consisting of millions of tiny particles of disbelief.

The gravitational force. Pulling, pulling, pulling critical structural connections toward the center of the earth.

The bursting inwards.

The violent collapse.

The implosion of a life—lived in great hopes of safe-happy-demanding-blessings-life-on-my-terms, more than a life lived in giving and being and eternal-loving, no matter the cost, in the reality of messy-living-dying-hurting-hard-awful-beautiful.

I will always show you where to go.
I'll give you a full life in the emptiest of places—
firm muscles, strong bones.
You'll be like a well-watered garden,
a gurgling spring that never runs dry.
You'll use the old rubble of past lives to build anew,
rebuild the foundations from out of your past.
You'll be known as those who can fix anything,
restore old ruins, rebuild and renovate,
make the community livable again.
—Isaiah 58:11-12, *The Message.*

Here is the world. Beautiful and terrible things will happen. Don't be afraid. Reach out and embrace His grace. Reach out and embrace Him. Nothing—not the death of your child, not cancer or other health calamities, not loneliness, not depression, not terror or anxiety, not sullied and stained relationships—nothing can separate us from God's eternal covenant of love.

We are not forsaken, even if we sometimes feel like it.

We are invited into the fullest of relational soul to relational soul life, in the emptiest of places.

You remember Your intentions for people, and You never lose sight of Your vision for the soul You intend to sculpt, and You never grow weak or weary in reinforcing the expression of that. What an honor that You would be our strength. Our eternal light. What an honor that You extend to us Invitation of the Most Precious Kind, long for us to join You, to know You, to love You, to love each other, in this holy, sacred, sacrificial place. Not as mere spectators of Your cross, but as alive-in-suffering-joy participants, giving our own body and blood in loving others.

This terrible beautiful place, where love has battled death with a passion fierce as the grave.

Postlude

"One life on this earth is all that we get,
whether it is enough or not enough, and the
obvious conclusion would seem to be that at the
very least we are fools if we do not live it as
fully and bravely and beautifully as we can."
—Frederick Buechner

T HESE ARE THE WORDS, LAYERED WITH meaning, that I have found for you, my
dear husband. *Schema of a Soul*, my
offering . . . to you.

I will never forget your young, engaging face from
that day I first met you, in the library.

What if I would have never met you?

It was about a year after that extraordinary day
when you presented to me a poem you had written for me.
You wrote it in blue ink on a sheet of regular-lined school
paper turned sideways, your lyrical words forming perfectly
shaped letters that spelled my name. KIM. I have protected
it in a plastic folder for forty years. I remember showing
it to Michael the day he showed me the one-hundred-piece
Thomas Kinkade puzzle he was writing on the back of for
Courtney. She was having a particularly challenging time
during the last week of an organic chemistry class. He

mailed her ten puzzle pieces every day for ten days. When she put it all together, she could read the entire message he had written on the back. Like your poem, it was full of encouragement and life-strengthening words. Lasting words. Enduring words. Sacred words...

You are the shared common denominator in my most profound stories of life and death and love. I wonder if you can know the richness, the deepness, the full-bodied impact you have had on my one precious life.

I want you to know.

Our love is no longer young, untried, untested, or naive. We are no longer young, untried, untested, or naive.

Growing wisdom wrings the naive right out of you in all of the hard-to-endure turmoil and all of the being-pushed-and-pulled-in-and-under strain.

For so long throughout the fallout of our tragedy we feared we would never be restored, regenerated, or redeemed. That it would never be well with our souls. Fully aware we never know what a day will bring, we know there will be the day that brings more. More pain. More tragedy. More turmoil. More death. While it is hard to even imagine, there will also be the day that brings the reality of no more pain, no more tears, no more death, but only the most joyful expressions of eternal life and love that will last forever.

So many moments we spent in puddles of tears together. My tears do not intimidate you anymore. I like that. I like the way you look me in the eye and gently begin a conversation. We have been soaking wet and all drenched in ugly together, but in our weeping we have been discovering the more that transcends the pain.

Ours is love that has battled death. A sustained, holy struggle. *"You thought you were being made into a decent little cottage: but He is building a palace. He intends to come and live in it Himself."*
—C. S. Lewis.

It is an awful and beautiful thing to be in process of
dying to all of the ways we selfishly defile love. You have
loved me and I have loved you in awful and in beautiful.
You'll use the old rubble of past lives to build
anew. Rebuild foundations from out of your past.
You'll be known as those who can fix anything,
restore old ruins, rebuild and renovate,
make the community livable again.
—*Isaiah 58:12, The Message.*

We are not ghosts. There is something solid forming
within each of us. Layer upon relational layer. Something
at our very core that will not be destroyed, no matter how
much more is to come. Love bears the pain with a joy previously unknown.

God has been building and restoring and regenerat-
ing and redeeming, and He intends to come and live in it
Himself.

The holy-overwhelming-interruption-God-given-
intense-impact-kairos-time...

He intends to live in us.

He invites us to live in Him.

Throughout our reconstruction, you have not lost
sight of the vision of the lives we are building and what it
means to reinforce the expression of that.

What is the life we are building?

It is, unquestionably, a life of love.

What does it mean to love each other in this place?

God is sculpting our souls to be alive-in-suffering-joy
participants in His cross, giving our own bodies and blood
in the endless ways you love me and I love you and we love
others...

That is what it means to love each other in this place.

Of course we are still messy, tangled, and tousled.
Life is not linear but wanders all untidy-like and can be
downright flummoxing. Full of frayed and loose ends and

mystery and untamed wildness and surprises, and it makes you vulnerable to dangers, and it can take all of your breath straight away.

It is enough, and it is not enough at all. Physical death is imminent for all of us. Seldom can you know when last words will come to you. But they will come. Let them be enduring words, sacred words...

What is there—but to live and love fully and bravely and beautifully in completely bound, secured, never-lets-go-fastened-together, unblinded, sacrificial love that is stronger than death?

The fullest of relational soul to relational soul life.

On earth.

And in heaven.

"His conversation is sweetness itself, He is alto-gether lovable. Such is my Beloved, such is my friend." —The Song of Songs 5:16, The Jerusalem Bible.

Set me like a seal on your heart, like a seal on your arm. For love is strong as Death, jealousy relentless as Sheol. The flash of it is a flash of fire, a flame of Yahweh himself. Love no flood can quench, no torrents drown. —The Song of Songs 8:6-7 The Jerusalem Bible.

"I can't believe I get you."

You, as my husband, my faithful friend, have made my life particularly deep and rich and colorful and layered with light and shadow and such intense gestalt beautiful I can barely breathe. I am coming to know God in places and in ways I would have never known without knowing you and living this one wild and precious life with you. You are the most full-of-grace person I have ever known. I would marry you again in a heartbeat. I am so grateful for our children and all of our life and death and love stories. I am so grateful for you. I am madly in love with you... Thank you for the library you designed for me. *"Are we not like two volumes of one book?"* *—Marceline Desbordes-Valmore.* I love meeting you there regularly. Especially in the glowing-beautiful of dawn and dusk... soul-stirring acoustics from beginning to end.

—Kim

CPSIA information can be obtained at www.ICGtesting.com
Printed in the USA
BVOW03s0538111113

335974BV00004B/7/P